NIETZSCHE AS EDUCATOR

Timothy F. Murphy

UNIVERSITY
PRESS OF
AMERICA

LANHAM • NEW YORK • LONDON

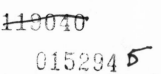

University Press of America,™ Inc.

4720 Boston Way
Lanham, MD 20706

3 Henrietta Street
London WC2E 8LU England

Library of Congress Cataloging in Publication Data

Murphy, Timothy F., 1955-
    Nietzsche as educator.

    1. Nietzsche, Friedrich Wilhelm, 1844-1900.
2. Education—Philosophy—History—19th century. I. Title.
B3317.M88   1984   193   84-2264
ISBN 0-8191-3839-8 (alk. paper)
ISBN 0-8191-3840-1 (pbk. : alk. paper)

for George P. Determan

A voice Said, Look me in the stars
And tell me truly, men of earth
If all the soul and body scars
Were not too much to pay for birth

Robert Frost

Acknowledgements

I would like to thank the people whose support was valuable during the writing and production of this book.

Richard Cobb-Stevens was my doctoral dissertation advisor at Boston College, and in that capacity provided much valued and appreciated support and direction when times called for clear and measured thinking. I am proud to be associated with him.

I would also like to thank those people who provided moral support during the production of this work: Lou Carroll, with whom I constantly disagree; James Chansky, who agreed with me when I needed to be agreed with; and Steven Scherwatzky, for being a ready listener.

Grateful acknowledgment is hereby made to the following for permission to use previously published material.

"A Question" from THE POETRY OF ROBERT FROST edited by Edward Connery Lathem. Copyright (c) 1942 by Robert Frost. Copyright (c) 1969 by Holt, Rinehart and Winston. Copyright (c) 1970 by Lesley Frost Ballantine. Reprinted by permission of Holt, Rinehart and Winston, Publishers.

From BEYOND GOOD AND EVIL by Friedrich Nietzsche. Edited and translated by Walter Kaufmann. New York: Random House, 1966. Copyright (c) 1967 by Random House. Reprinted by permission of Random House, Inc.

From DAYBREAK by Friedrich Nietzsche, translated by R.J. Hollingdale. Cambridge: Cambridge University Press, 1982. Reprinted by permission of Cambridge University Press. Copyright (c) 1980 by Cambridge University Press.

From ECCE HOMO by Friedrich Nietzsche. Edited and translated by Walter Kaufmann. New YorK: Random House, 1969. Copyright (c) by Random House. Reprinted by permission of Random House, Inc.

From PHILOSOPHY AND TRUTH, SELECTIONS FROM NIETZSCHE'S NOTEBOOKS OF THE EARLY 1870'S, edited and translated by Daniel Breazeale. Copyright (c)1979 by Humanities Press. Reprinted by permission of

> And even then I am frightened by the
> thought of what unqualified and
> unsuitable people may invoke my
> authority one day. Yet that is the
> torment of every great teacher of
> mankind: he knows that given the
> circumstances and the accidents he
> can become a disaster as well as
> a blessing to mankind.
>
> Nietzsche (1)

In current histories of the philosophy of education there is a decided agreement on who constitute the pivotal figures in educational theory: Plato, Locke, Rousseau, for example. In those same volumes it happens that Nietzsche rarely receives any treatment at all, or if he is mentioned it is (a) to emphasize some point by quoting one of his trenchant remarks, or (b) to indicate merely that he authored the posthumously published "On the Future of Our Educational Institutions." In the latter case, these lectures are only mentioned in passing, stating the insistence Nietzsche places on educating the higher specimens of humanity and his contention that properly speaking education belongs only to them. In either case, however, these treatments are only obiter dicta and do not dwell on the nature of Nietzsche's concerns with education. (2)

This lack of concern seems odd given that Nietzsche was himself a university professor in the highly scholarly field of philology, that he makes numerous criticisms of university instruction and of scholars generally, and that his writing can often only be understood in terms of their educational import, this latter element being particularly evident in the central Thus Spoke Zarathustra. Nietzsche's entire corpus of works centers around, of course, the relationship between life and values. And in that respect his concerns would be those of a grand teacher (and this is not necessarily equatable with a grand scholar) who attempts through his criticism and example, to instruct humanity in a way to live. It would seem, moreover, that his very notion of philosophy cannot be understood but as being educative in nature. His specific aim is to alert humanity to and help humanity to avoid and overcome nihilism and decadence.

1

Most interpreters of Nietzsche ignore the primal position that education plays in his thought and, accordingly, it seems to me, do damage to his concern with the central role and essential nature of his conception of the genuine philosopher and philosophical activity. Even if Nietzsche does not merit a great deal of space in histories of philosophy of education since he, in fact, has not seemed to have much impact in the written accounts of educational theory, surely he deserves the attention necessary to attain an understanding of the nature, aims, and methods of his concern with education since these are intimately tied to his notion of philosophy. This project does not attempt to locate Nietzsche within the history of philosophies of education. Rather, what is attempted is a conceptual architecture of the issues that would be pertinent to such an endeavor.

This analysis attempts to show how Nietzsche considered himself as a teacher in the art of human living and how this teaching must proceed. Such a perspective provides a powerful way of reconciling the various threads of his wide-ranging writings (without claiming that this is a definitive interpretation; it will be seen why, for an important reason, there can be no definitive interpretation of Nietzsche). Construing men as self-creative beings, he exhorts men to be responsible for their own destinies. He advocates experiment with life, life becoming even the criterion of truth, goodness, and beauty. Towards the possibility of human experiment in life, he instructs in the art of living, and indeed he would seem to make philosophy itself responsible for this instruction.

Thus, Nietzsche intimately ties philosophy and education together. By giving a critique of existing social institutions and reigning values which impede experimentalism with life, Nietzsche criticizes the institutions, process, and product of contemporary education. Moreover, he criticizes the failure of philosophy to provide viable alternatives to the existing ways of living/learning. Nietzsche, as is well known, is concerned with the values of man. His reflections on those values give, both explicitly and implicitly, answers to other human questions. His posture on education is of a piece with his moral concerns. The rescue of man could come through the reform of philosophy concerned actively with the art of living.

Briefly, my argument moves from a consideration of Nietzsche's notion of philosophy through a consideration of the institutions and practices of education, to an examination of his proposed end of genuine philosophical education. His final proposal of genuine education is given in the language of the dance. This imagery of dancing symbolizes, for Nietzsche, the achievement of genuine education. 'Teaching the Dance' would be an appropriate subtitle of this book because Nietzsche's philosophic, moral and educational concerns merge in the

2

meaningful, vital and beautiful symbol and reality of the dance. In what follows here, I give a chapter by chapter overview of the book.

Chapter 1: The Character of Philosophy

    Nietzsche is considered a philosopher by many because he engages in activities typically taken to be 'philosophical,' for example, metaphysics and analytic philosophy. By reviewing the basic kind of argument for each claim ('Nietzsche is a philosopher because he does such and such.'), it is seen that these interpretations, while fruitful in themselves, ignore the value Nietzsche placed on teaching men how to live and, more specifically, how to live as man. Towards this end, it is contended here, all other philosophical activities are but means. Nietzsche deprecates philosophers who take metaphysics epistemology, or even logic as the essence of philosophical activity. These are for him no ends in themselves but means towards higher life although this conception of higher life must remain somewhat vague, conceived as it is in terms of human creativity. These activities are necessary, to be sure, but they do not constitute the end of philosophical activity. The lessons of Nietzsche's own metaphysics for that matter are of no small benefit to human advancement, whether personal or cultural, but they are never to be mistaken for the whole of education's task, for the culmination of human creativity.   The benefits of philosophical labors ought to be translated back into the human task of creativity. Nietzsche's own style and his remarks on the philosophical task show, via educative example, that the assessment of human accomplishment as a foundation for human creativity is the genuine task of the philosopher.

Chapter 2: Nietzsche on Education

    Though he preaches creativity and affirmation, it is evident in the most cursory of Nietzsche's writings that his tone is decidedly negative and destructive. When he turns his no-saying towards existing academic institutions and educational practices, it is for their failure to integrate the philosophical activities of the academy into a harmoniously constructed whole aiming at the education of man as a whole and the possibility of the overman in particular. Nietzsche's extensive criticism of existing social institutions is to be understood in terms of its failure to comply with this educational/philosophical task. Current schools do not educate in the etymological sense of 'to lead out,' but simply process human beings for their adequate participation in currently existing social compacts. He rejects the ideal of scholarship, the control of the state and science, and scores the foundational philosophy of these institutions. Contemporary education produces caricatures of human beings locked into professorialism or technicism. Counterposed to this state of affairs, Nietzsche offers the ethic of <u>amor</u> <u>fati</u> with its ethic of

3

creativity, an ethic which has implications well beyond the practice of schools but certainly implies repudiation of some of its most important, current practices.

Chapter 3: The Contest and Education

Nietzsche's writings are patently aimed at the few, and his theory of education is no less so (although there is an undeniable public intent behind Nietzsche). Continuing the discussion of the process of education begun in the previous chapter, this chapter takes up the notion of the contest as the pivotal element of educational practice. Nietzsche makes the <u>agon</u> the cornerstone of human struggle and philosophical advancement, thereby hallowing the contest as the test and expression of human power. Thus is to be understood the decidedly one-way relations that exist between Zarathustra and his disciples. Zarathustra, eager at first for listeners, rushes headlong into the marketplace only to learn that the humans gathered there have little ability to understand his talk of the overman, of the will to power, of the eternal return. Only after this defeat born of naivete does Zarathustra himself realize that wisdom or enlightenment cannot be achieved solely by the zeal of the teacher or the inherent importance of the message alone. Though he remains in a kind of contact with them, the rest of the book shows Zarathustra increasingly retreating from his students/disciples. If they are to understand him, it must be through struggling to understand themselves. They must assume the burden of education.

The contest is a <u>constructive</u> battle, in keeping with Nietzsche's position that there is no truth, only interpretation. For the contest <u>means</u> repudiation and surpassing of the teacher by the student, because Nietzsche has charged the student with the task of <u>amor</u> <u>fati</u>: become what you are, not what someone else, the state or science would make of you. Nietzsche would have the teacher initiate the student into the struggle for the kinds of experiential knowledge which allow the student the highest form of human living, living as creative man. The teacher and the student are thus locked into a contest, pitting themselves against one another in order to achieve their highest level of masteries (these being the conditions for the highest level of creation). In Nietzsche's own life, the desire for followers and the demanded renunciation of students generated a tension which expressed itself ambiguously. Nonetheless, the contest as the pivotal concept of educational process demands repudiation of the teacher by the student in the name of creativity.

Chapter 4: The Teacher and The Lie

Continuing the line of discussion developed with reference to the educational process of the continual contest, the lie and the mask become important to consider for their relation to the teacher and student as well as to life itself. It might almost

4

seem contradictory for Nietzsche to arrogate to the teacher the right to lie when he so inexorably denounces religion's use of the lie. Beyond this simple contradiction, it might seem wrong for Nietzsche to advocate the use of the lie or mask at all for its apparent opposition to his stated goal of honesty and truthfulness in all things. Yet, this chapter rehearses an argument that the lie and mask are important to human achievement and the possibility of life at all. Most people are honest, he cynically remarks, because they are not intelligent enough to coordinate their lies and, so, get caught in them. Falsehood is not objected to in itself, then, but only because of possible consequences. Nietzsche moves to show that the mask and lie, in the contest between student and teacher, are not purely instruments of deception. Lies and masks perpetuate the context while at the same time preservng a distinction between superficial and profound truth. The creative individual, moreover, would almost have to speak in the language of lies, since falsity is measured against the ordained conventions of 'truth.' Lies and masks are necessary for life in that they provide horizons of meaning for human action and conduct. Since there are no truths, man must be a liar, must use masks in order to live. To reconcile these lies and masks with ultimately intellectual probity, Nietzsche would have man never forget that they are only lies, only masks.

Chapter 5: Teaching the Dance

With the review of Nietzsche's examination of institution and process of education complete, we are in a position to examine his idea of its product. Nietzsche symbolized the educational/philosophical ideal in the dance, a frequent image throughout his works. The dance combines with the symbol of playing to reflect the highest will to power. The dance escapes the criticisms Nietzsche makes of contemporary education and embodies the contest he suggests as educative process. Moreover, just as the individual dances so can a civilization, so can a universe.

In all these cases, the use of the symbol remains the same: unification of divergent strains and impulses into a mastered, creative activity, this being the locus of human meaning itself. The aim of education is precisely this on all levels; the dance of men set in the context of the dance of the eternal return. The dance transforms the lessons of the past, achievements both intellectual and moral into the meaning of life.

With this work I do not wish to claim that other interpreters have failed to understand Nietzsche. I wish rather to restore a sense of Nietzsche as educator to primacy when we think about him. I find the image of the philosopher/educator teaching the dance a compelling one. Mind and body, achievement and possibility, unity and divergence, power and beauty, will and instinct are united in the symbol and reality of the dance.

It is no surprise that after a certain eclipse Nietzsche has been beset by 'scholarly oxen,' for his writings provide a wealth of scholarly riches. I would like with this book to have shown the one-sidedness of merely intellectual philosophy. Nietzsche knew well the cost of thought that liberated. He knew well, too, the history of those who fail to make the decisive step from mere thought to meaningfulness. I would like to have shown that the true educator's task, the true philosopher's task must confront human meaning as a lived problem. Nietzsche is an exemplary philosopher in this respect. The nature of his solution, the dance, is, I believe, a major step from mere thought to authentic human meaning.

Chapter 1

THE CHARACTER OF PHILOSOPHY

> ...for Axioms in philosophy are
> not axioms until they are proved
> upon our pulses: We read fine
> things but never feel them to the
> full until we have gone the same
> steps as the Author.
>
> Keats (1)

In one of his earliest publications, Nietzsche considered Schopenhauer as educator. It is the case that Nietzsche receives infrequent mention in the histories of the philosophy of education, and it is glaringly obvious that Schopenhauer receives virtually no mention. By what logic did Nietzsche understand Schopehauer as Erzieher? The answer shows philosophy as inherently educative in character. For example, Nietzsche remarks about his discussion of Schopenhauer that:

> it is not nearly enough if I merely paint
> an imperfect picture of the ideal man who
> rules in and around Schopenhauer, as his
> Platonic ideal, so to speak. The most
> difficult task still remains: to say how
> a new sphere of duties is to be gained
> from this ideal and how one can obtain such
> a lofty goal through regular activity,
> in short, to prove that this ideal
> educates. (SE, 49)

Taking this remark as the starting point for this investigation, what follows is an attempt to show that understanding Nietzsche as a philosopher simply because he is a metaphysician, say, ignores his efforts to measure philosophical cogency against actual lived practice. In brief, to be a philosopher means, for Nietzsche, being a visionary, a teacher, and an example. If Nietzsche attempts an assessment of Schopenhauer's philosophy by examining its educative potential, then it does not seem wrong-headed to understand Nietzsche as a philosopher interested in education. Moreover, as will be seen throughout, both the manner and content of Nietzsche's discussions show him to be actively concerned about the educative aspects of philosophical positions.

To use Nietzsche's own formula of assessment, one wonders

7

what new sphere of duties Nietzsche imposed, what lofty goal Nietzsche as educator proposed. The answers to these questions constitute the five subsequent chapters. What did Nietzsche expect of the universities? What is the meaning of the contest that he so insisted on? What is the role of masks and lies in his vision? Why does his vision take the dance as symbol? In brief, this essay constructs a conceptual architecture of the issues pertinent to considering Nietzsche as educator. There are many ways to approach Nietzsche, and I do not claim to be promulgating the definitive approach. I want to suggest a way of reading him which is sympathetic to and attempts to make sense of his widely scattered remarks on education, the nature of his style, and the vision so often expressed in symbols. The key to this interpretation is understanding Nietzsche as a philosopher because of his educative enterprise. His notion of philosophy is tied to the very concept of education.

There have been many interpreters of Nietzsche who have followed out one aspect of his thought, trying to present Nietzsche's position on a given subject. While such endeavors are fruitful for their systematic consideration, these interpretations have often been unfair to Nietzsche's overall intent. Consequently, a one-sided version of Nietzsche often emerges at the hands of these writers. Most importantly, it seems to me that Nietzsche's very conception of philosophy has been damaged in this fashion. Most interpreters understand Nietzsche as a philosopher at all because he engages in metaphysics, epistemology, value theory, or even analytic philosophy. It will be seen that most commentators on Nietzsche's claim to the title of philosopher rely on his metaphysical abilities (Heidegger, Kaufmann, and Alderman). Two interpreters say Nietzsche is a philosopher because of his Socratic quest for knowledge of how to live (Neumann, Fischer). What I say of these authors applies a fortiori to other commentators not mentioned here. I hope to show that in light of Nietzsche's own remarks and manner that the above interpreters present (whatever else their merits) a one-sided account which ignores or discounts the educative aspect of philosophy. By judging Nietzsche by his own definition of philosopher, it is seen that he is eminently entitled to consideration and stature as a philosopher of education. Towards the end of teaching man (understanding man here as the aristocratically exemplary human) how to live, epistemology, language analysis, and metaphysics are instruments of the philosophical task, not in themselves the whole of philosophy.

This does not mean that metaphysics, epistemology, and the rest are in any way disvalued. On the contrary, they are all necessary activities both in historical and personal development. It is to say, however, that no one of these activities defines the concept of philosophy. They may be necessary conditions of the philosophical life, but they are not sufficient conditions. And

8

Nietzsche would add that in order to be genuine philosophy, these activities must instruct in how to live well, to live creatively. Only then has philosophy completed its appointed task, only then has it educated.

A procedural ambiguity should be addressed here. There are three ways in which one might approach my thesis. First, one might review the commentators for their opinions and then move on to a critical examination of Nietzsche's writings for support of the thesis. This procedure has the defect of leaving the bulk of the evidence for noting difficulties with the commentators' views until well after those views have been discussed. The second manner might put the evidence for Nietzsche as educator first and then move to a review of the commentators. This procedure moves to establish a thesis before it has been shown that anyone does or does not hold such and such views. It also makes the review of the commentators anti-climactic and tedious. The third manner might be to discuss the thesis and commentators together. However, this procedure suffers from the scattershot approach and spreads the arguments out over too long a time. The discussion that follows here does, in fact, take the first format indicated. Hopefully, acknowledging its shortcomings in advance will serve to mitigate them, although it cannot hope to eliminate them. In the long run, this format seemed to best organize the argument.

As a final preliminary remark, it will be seen that some response is made to each commentator discussed. However, this discussion is rather limited. It is neither necessary nor desirable to go into a full assessment of the cogency of the full argument presented. The Main ask centers on showing how education has a central status in Nietzsche's conception and living of philosophy.

The order of discussion of the various commentators on Nietzsche will proceed thus: Martin Heidegger, Walter Kaufmann, Arthur Danto, Frederick Copleston, and Harold Alderman. The first authors, Heidegger, Kaufmann, Danto, and Copleston, provide the basic paradigms which are pertinent to the first half of this chapter's thesis. Each of these philosophers calls Nietzsche a philosopher because of his metaphysical formulations, and they all call attention in one way or another to his axiological concerns. Copleston and Danto, moreover, attempt to show the link between Nietzsche and analytic philosophy. Harold Alderman does raise the issue of education/teaching in his relatively recent book, and his discussion provides the entrée into the review of Nietzsche proper. As noted, other commentators will not be considered since their arguments are of a piece with the foregoing analyses.

The sum and substance of Heidegger's approach to Nietzsche is quite clearly stated in the first three sections of his Nietzsche. In the first place, Heidegger insists on the primacy of Nietzsche's unpublished notes in his interpretation, (2) arguing that the published works are minimized by the fact that as published they have only the incidental value of foreground philosophy. (3) Heidegger proposes on such a basis to give an understanding of Nietzsche that shows Nietzsche as the heir and culmination of the wrongly-posed question of Western metaphysics. It is justly said that "Heidegger regards Nietzsche primarily as a metaphysician and treats all other aspects of his philosophy as systematically derivative from his metaphysics.(4) Heidegger says of his subject that he follows the guiding question of philosophy, "What is being?" (5) That Nietzsche follows the mainstream of Western thought, however, does not diminish his importance, to be sure: "the reference to the fact that Nietzsche moves in the orbit of the question of Western philosophy only serves to make it clear that Nietzsche knew what philosophy is.   Such knowledge is rare."(6)

But beyond placing Nietzsche in the Western tradition of thought, which is not particularly problematic at all, Heidegger attempts to appropriate Nietzsche for his own assessment of that tradition:

> The task of our lecture course is to
> elucidate the fundamental position within
> which Nietzsche unfolds the guiding question
> of Western thought and responds to it.
> Such elucidation is needed in order to
> prepare a confrontation with Nietzsche.
> If in Nietzsche's thinking the prior
> tradition of Western thought is gathered
> and completed in a decisive aspect, then
> the confrontation with Nietzsche becomes
> one with all Western thought hitherto. (7)

Heidegger plans to show Nietzsche as a kind of culmination and end of the orientation of Western philosophy.

One might say that Heidegger is concerning himself with a theory of truth. Rejecting the prevalent subject/object model of knowing (which attempts to establish the veracity of the relationship between mental representations and the empirical, objective world), Heidegger proposes an alternative model of human knowing. He questions the notion of being as res, understood as a matter of objectivity, and recasts the question of knowing in terms of intentionality. He thus bypasses the question of the possibility of the interior conditions of objectivity. He attempts to show that to be an intentional being is to be within

10

being by reason of an a prior condition. So considered, intentionaly, now an ontological category rater than an epistemological category, becomes a dimension of being itself (as opposed to a particular being). 'Truth,' then, is neither a matter of a fully apprised relationship between representations and their objects, nor a function of the mind's interiority. Heidegger proposes to retrieve what he claims to be a Greek, pre-epistemological understnding of truth. Heidegger turns to the question of meaning in order to show that truth is neither a purely empirical event nor simply a matter of transcendental categories of understanding. The crux of Heidegger's judgment of Nietzsche can, then, be easily seen: insofar as Nietzsche claimed there was no truth, he was demonstrating the impoverishment of the basic metaphysical model of the theory of truth in Western philosophy. In this way, Nietzsche stood as a kind of end, albeit a destructive one, of Western metaphysics.

It should be obvious that an assessment of these kinds of claims would substantially detract from the emphasis of this essay. Heidegger's approach to and conclusions about Nietzsche are quite controversial. It does not seem to me that to sidestep this controversy detracts from my thesis here in general or in any particulars, namely the attempt to elucidate the nature of the philosophic task according to Nietzsche, an endeavor which must be undertaken with many blinders in order to see clearly the text and meaning of Nietzsche. It is my opinion that when reading Heidegger on Nietzsche, it is well to keep in mind Nietzsche's own realization about his book on Schopenhauer: this was a book about Nietzsche, not Schopenhauer. It suffices to say, therefore, that Heidegger thought Nietzsche a philosopher for his abiding metaphysical interest and accomplishments (even if these signified denial of the possibility of metaphysics as construed in the Western tradition). (8)

Kaufmann, one of the principle expositors of Nietzsche in America, holds that Nietzsche was a philosopher even though he was not a systematic philosopher in the style of Hegel or Spinoza. Kaufmann says of Nietzsche's method that in spite of all the apparent contradictions one can see that Nietzsche did "attain a philosophy." (9) Further, he says that Nietzsche's aphoristic style does, in fact, "add up to a philosophy," (10) and this in spite of the fact that he had no system per se. Kaufmann holds this position because he thinks Nietzsche is a problem thinker, a philosopher who tackles individual problems, and whose specific virtue as such is refusing to accept any system premises as beyond question, as inexorably true. Yet what can Kaufmann mean by holding that Nietzsche's writings "add up" to a philosophy? It can only mean that Nietzsche established a structure of interpretation which was capable of responding to or making sense of all the facets of human experience, at least in principle if not in fact. It would seem, then, that although Kaufmann

11

identifies Nietzsche as a problem-thinker (as distinguished from a system thinker) nevertheless, in maintaining that his works add up to a philosophy, they add up to a system. Now, it would be well to look further at the kinds of results that Kaufmann finds issuing from Nietzsche's endeavors. For it will be seen that Kaufmann is implicitly representing Nietzsche's methodology as philosophy for its metaphysically explanatory powers (even though perhaps only as tentatively explanatory).

Kaufmann maintains that though he did not want a system, Nietzsche did want philosophy to become scientific, wissenschaftliche, not on the order of Hegelian or Kantian philosophical 'scientism,' but as a 'gay science' "of fearless experiment and the good will to accept new evidence and to abandon previous positions, if necessary." (11)   Such a conception of "scientific" is markedly different from that of a Hegel to be sure. Kaufmann correctly names existential experimentalism as the core of this science, but in the long run the difference is so great that it is perhaps misleading to think of Nietzsche's as a scientific philosophy, even a 'gay' science, for the reason that if the premises and basic assumptions in structures of interpretations are always subject to change, even welcome change, then one cannot attempt to achieve the kind of necessity in statement and results that is the professed ideal of scientific endeavor and presumed goal of metaphysical analysis.   That Nietzsche is an experimentalist is readily granted; however, to infer from this a kind of 'scientism' seems misleading since, as will be shown, Nietzsche's is ultimately a metaphysics of creativity rather than a metaphysics modeled on 'scientific' understanding.

As indicated, Kaufmann points out that the problems which require experiment have a strong existential component motivating them.   (This is the basis of Neumann's comparison of Nietzsche and Socrates: "Both raise the question of what is good for himself." (30)) This limits for each individual the number of philosophical questions or problems that one will face, according to one's own life situation. He says quite rightly, too, that:

> Inquiry must take for its starting point a
> problem that is concrete and not artificial
> or merely 'academic.' (12)

Kaufmann quotes Nietzsche to the effect that both science and philosophy must proceed with an eye towards the concrete lived experience of human beings. (13) They must never stray into the bloodless realm of pure speculation or abstraction. Kaufmann then goes on to remark about the value of 'systematizing,' its value in showing contradictions and inconsistencies, this without claiming that any lack of such faults guarantees the ultimate truth of any system. He criticizes Nietzsche on this score:

...while offering many fruitful hypotheses
Nietzsche failed to see that only a systematic
attempt to substantiate them could establish
am impressive probability in their favor. (14)

Such a criticism does not, it seems, speak to Nietzsche's own
characterization of philosophy; it retains as far as possible
traditional, systematic standards of philosophical thinking,
namely the rational solving of problems in such a way as to make
them compatible with solutions to other problems. Either problem
thinking is just limited system thinking or Kaufmann is testing
Nietzsche against the system standard without being explicit on
that count. In other words, Kaufmann does not offer any remarks
as to why questions and problems born of lived experience require
'systematic' substantiation unless, of course, one is trying to
establish a system.

Kaufmann does make provision for the existential character
of this problem solving, but this does not prevent him from
evaluating Nietzsche on grounds of metaphysical rationality as the
criterion of evaluation. And by calling Nietzsche's mode of
philosophy 'scientific,' Kaufmann continues to perpetuate reason
as a criterion of truth, a position that Nietzsche vehemently
resisted. Nietzsche substitutes will to power as the criterion of
truth, and it is not established beforehand that contradictions
and inconsistencies impede the exercise, the truth of power.
Indeed, it might even be the case that the ability to live in a
contradictory manner might even advance one's power. Ambiguity
might require more power than systematized truth. In any case,
the contradictions and inconsistencies that reason points out
might not be such when measured against a criterion of life (read:
power). Kaufmann's criticism can only be understood, it seems, in
the context of attempting to systematize. Such a treatment
enables him to conclude that Nietzsche's writings "add up" to a
philosophy, namely they add up to a system. Yet if the will to
system is a lack of integrity, as Nietzsche announces (and
Kaufmann quotes him on this) (15), then Kaufmann would seem to
have disregarded Nietzsche's own dictum with respect to the proper
method of philosophy. This is not to say that Nietzsche's ideas
are incompatible when taken as a whole, or that they are
inherently contradictory; but it is to say that it is unfair to
assess Nietzsche on the grounds of rationality (with its attendant
demand for coherence and consistency) which Nietzsche continually
images as impoverished with respect to the full scope of
philosophy. Thus, while Kaufmann does talk about Nietzsche's
method and makes some remarks about its intent, he does not
explicitly address the nature of Nietzsche's philosophizing. That
is he discusses its methodology but not the full implications for
the nature of philosophy.

13

The very title, <u>Nietzsche as Philosopher</u>, suggests a certain novelty in considering Nietzsche as a philosopher. In this work, Danto approaches Nietzsche from the viewpoint of analytic philosophy and decides that Nietzsche <u>is</u> genuinely a philosopher. Danto identifies Nietzsche's purpose as attempting to crack the habitual grip in which language holds us, to make us aware of how much our minds are dominated by concepts, to create fresh concepts and so whole new philosophies. (16) To effect such a liberation, Nietzsche attacks the scarcely acknowledged conceptual foundations of our existence: "It is for this that he is entitled to be called a philosopher." (17)

On the very same page, Danto then goes on to say that Nietzsche is more than a critic of concepts: he tried to construct an entire philosophy. On the one hand, Danto claims Nietzsche as a philosopher because he focussed critical reflection on the conceptual architecture of human life. But on the other hand, Danto implies that philosophy is something beyond the analytic enterprise, i.e., something beyond conceptual analysis. One can find, he says, that Nietzsche is almost "a systematic as well as an original and analytic thinker" if "one takes the trouble to eke his philosophy out." (18) This seems to mean that conceptual thinking becomes philosophical thinking when applied metaphysically, i.e., as claims about man and world. Although I am not convinced that Danto is entirely aware of what he is doing, he does identify Nietzsche's philosophical activities here as conceptual examination <u>and</u> metaphysics.

As to the former activity, it is well to keep in mind Danto's remark: "I have not hesitated to reconstruct Nietzsche's argument in these [analytic] terms, when this was compatible with the aim of making a book available to the general reader." (19) Noting further that Nietzsche has not influenced analytic philosophy, he says: "it is for the movement to reclaim him as a philosopher." (20) Certainly, these statements show Danto's methodology to be concerned with rehabilitating Nietzsche as an analytic thinker. One can expect to find therefore no attention paid to the issue of what made Nietzsche think himself a philosopher. In the course of the book, Danto treats Nietzsche as he states, as an analytic and, to a less explicit extent, as a metaphysical thinker. Such an enterprise is not without merit, to be sure; nevertheless, I shall argue that the intention of Nietzsche's philosophizing goes beyond these aims.

Another popularizer and interpreter of Nietzsche, Copleston, also decides that Nietzsche is a philosopher because he is a metaphysician, even if he is a very bad one. (21) Copleston asserts this of Nietzsche because the latter is telling us what the world is like <u>really</u>, metaphysically, even though it would seem that his is a kind of empirical, inductive metaphysics. Copleston finds a contradiction in Nietzsche's maintaining that

14

all truths are ultimately fictions (in the sense of being the product of interpretations) and Nietzsche's claiming to tell what the world is like in itself even if it seems that he is doing so mytho-morally. (22)

The privileged position that Nietzsche's interpretation seems to hold with respect to all other interpretations raises some interesting and important questions. Is Nietzsche's position unlike other interpretations? Is his exhortation to creativity metaphysically more valid than other interpretations? And if so, how does one measure that validity? What if someone in a competing interpretation claims that that interpretation offers a greater condition of human freedom? How do we choose between them and at the same time not violate Nietzsche's precept that his is no more than one interpretation among many? At first blush, it would seem that Nietzsche is guilty of an inconsistency, that his position metaphysically describes, as Copleston maintains, what the world and man are like in themselves. On the other hand, I do not find that Nietzsche ever actively ascribes a metaphysical character to his position such that it is ultimately true beyond any possible revision. The apparent inconsistency seems to arise from the functional quality of Nietzsche's position as meta-descriptive of human knowing and interpretation. That his position claims that all human knowing is an interpretation does not, eo ipso, mean that his position is not an interpretation. One can argue that his meta-level analysis is still very much an interpretation. To account for its validity, however, one has to ask what makes it truer than its competing interpretations. At this point, the issue turns into a question of the validity of Nietzsche's overall criticisms of metaphysics. I decline to take upthis matter fully here since to do so would shift the emphasis from Nietzsche as educator to Nietzsche as epistemologist. (23)

In a second consideration, Copleston ponders the value of Nietzsche in regard to "philosophy as we know it in this country," in regard to language analysis. (24) Claiming that Nietzsche is a great questioner, Copleston remarks that:

> My point is that reflecting on Nietzsche's
> questioning is not a bad way of immersing
> oneself in philosophical problems and of
> examining the limits of the sayable and the
> thinkable. The activity may not attract
> everyone. But it seems to be a reasonably
> respectable form of critical reflection. (25)

Nietzsche does explore the limits of the expressible. I do not think, however, that such a characterization does completely adumbrates his conception of philosophy. What has been established here though is that Copleston finds both metaphysics and linguistic analysis in Nietzsche and therefore he concludes that he is philosopher. Copleston's primary interpretation of Nietzsche is of a piece with those of Kaufmann and Heidegger since, it, too, classifies Nietzsche as a philosopher since he attempts, however tentatively and experimentally, metaphysics.

There is one commentator, Harold Alderman, who specifically examines Nietzsche at the metaphilosophical level. In Nietzsche's Gift, Alderman ask about Nietzsche's conception of philosophy: what is it that makes him a philosopher? His answer:

> Nietzsche's work is quintessentially and
> fundamentally philosophical exactly because
> it focuses on the origin, structure, and
> limitation of human thought and experience. (26)

The claim that Nietzsche is a philosopher because he reflects on the nature of human thought we have seen before. However, Alderman enlarges the claim to include the entire gamut of human experience. I wonder if this definition is not too broad: if one is not examining the origin, structure and limitation of human thought and experience, what else could one possibly be examining? Apart from the objects of natural science, is there study outside these categories which would make one not a philosopher? It can be agreed with Alderman that Nietzsche was first and foremost a philosopher and even that he was perhaps the first and foremost philosopher of philosophy, (27) but the claim that establishes Nietzsche as fundamentally a philosopher would also seem to make everyone a philosopher, in which case Alderman has scarcely done Nietzsche any service.

It is the contention of this essay that Nietzsche is a philosopher insofar as he engages in educative activity that promotes the ascending power of the human condition and this is how Nietzsche himself considered himself to be a philosopher. That Nietzsche does focus on all the things that Alderman considers is not denied; indeed, such analyses as Nietzsche makes are invaluable in the service of his whole enterprise. But I hope to show they do not, for all that, constitute him as a philosopher on his own grounds. They remain philosophical labors of metaphysics, epistemology, and the rest. They are not the end of philosophy itself.

Later in his book, Alderman asserts that "Nietzsche's work is quintessentially philosophical because of its transcendental exploration of the foundations of experience." (28) Further, Nietzsche reintroduces the interiority of experience into thought. (29) While these things, too, are quite true, they do not go far enough. Nietzsche is not making reflection or analysis per se of the human condition the object of his philosophical endeavors; neither is he simply reintroducing the interiority of experience

16

into the analysis of human life. As a philosopher, he attempts to do these things, yes, but I take it that the point is not to remain at the level of pure reflection, but to return these assessments to the realm of life such that they make a difference there. Thus, when Alderman says of the Birth of Tragedy that it is not primarily a work of philosophy, (30) this is the result of his not assuming Nietzsche's own conception of philosophy according to which the analysis of tragedy is a spur to life. Alderman is sensitive in realizing that Nietzsche's writings cannot be evaluated according to the traditional dictates of philosophical analysis. According to such standards, he says, it would appear that Part IV of Thus Spoke Zarathustra seems superfluous and redundant.

> That is, however, a criterion of superfluity
> which simply assumes the traditional conception
> of philosophy as theory—as detached, objective
> spectatorship. But as I have argued, one of the
> most important elements of the philosophical
> revolution accomplished by Nietzsche is the
> introduction of the idea that beyond reason and
> theories there is the vita—and still philo-
> sophical—realm of experience and belief which
> transcends but is not disconnected from reasons
> and theories. (31)

It is odd, given this reflection, that Alderman does not consider the conception of Dionysus in the Birth of Tragedy as a philosophical ideal, as an idea beyond the pale of Apollinian categories.

Although Alderman himself warns that Nietzsche's writings cannot be reviewed entirely dispassionately and disinterestedly, he still makes evaluations of Nietzsche's books in a manner that does damage to Nietzsche's conception of their possible instrumentality for life. Alderman ranks the books according to their philosophical value and concludes: "In comparison to Thus Spoke Zarathustra, all of Nietzsche's other books, with the possible exception of Beyond Good and Evil, become philosophically secondary — although not in many respects, uninteresting." (32) However, as with his judgment on the Birth of Tragedy, this kind of evaluation assumes that there is one way of getting at all the exploration via this book, namely as if all the relevant doctrines were stated in Zarathustra and merely repeated elsewhere. However, if a book cannot be a thing-in-itself, as Alderman himself argues, (33) then an entire philosophical corpus cannot be reduced to a single-most important text. If Nietzsche's writing does have a poetic-fictive character to it, a dramatic character, then certainly the form of the drama has meaning. And since Zarathustra is not the entire drama of Nietzsche, then it cannot be considered as the entire story, philosophically speaking. It seems a mistake to dismiss as secondary the very thing that Nietzsche took so seriously later in his life, namely the revaluation of values, an enterprise which Zarathustra cannot be said to repeat or entirely foreshadow.

Finally, in light of Alderman's own repudiation of the idea of the book-in-itself and his own recognition of the value of the dramatic structure of writing, making a judgment on Zarathustra as the most important book of Nietzsche's would be similar to claiming that Wordsworth's most important book is "Ode: Intimations of Immortality" because it prefigures and contains the basic Wordsworthian themes. Surely, one would not want to do this to the Wordsworth corpus. One wonders too whether Alderman would maintain that in the other works, Nietzsche did not engage in transcendental exploration of experience, his primary criterion for establishing a work as philosophical.

Alderman wants to put Nietzsche "in the very first rank of those major philosophers who necessarily take the nature of philosophy as an item of their primary concern." (34) Alderman thus remarks:

> Thus this book is only a recommendation—
> that is all any interpretation is—to read
> Nietzsche in a certain way that frees
> his thought from merely literary,
> psychological, biographical or historical
> modes of interpretation, so that his books
> may be read as the most philosophical
> about the nature of philosophy. (35)

I would suggest that in so fracturing Nietzsche's work, we would commit the very kind of error that Nietzsche thought philosophy had perpetuated since Plato, namely the dissociation of thought from the ground of life. Nietzsche liberally spices his books with literary, psychological, biographical, and historical remarks and analyses. His whole Ecce Homo is a kind of autobiographical psychical history. To "free" evaluations of Nietzsche from this ground seems curiously misdirected given Nietzsche's own indulgence in straying from academic philosophy. Moreover, it seems to me the imposition of categories which are strictly historical, biographical, psychological, etc., does damage to the very enterprise that Nietzsche was launching in order to break down those artificial categories, born of academic division of labor, in order to bring them all to bear in the life of the noble human being in a manner that is not crippling or caricaturing.

In many ways, the most important aspect of Alderman's book is his anlysis of Nietzsche's notion of will to power, an anlysis which departs from either Heidegger's or Kaufmann's. However, for purposes of this effort we must limit ourselves to the claims about Nietzsche's status as a philosopher, not with the particular philosophical doctrines attributed to him.

The editor of a recent, large encyclopedia of education point out that in one sense, all experience is educative, such that almost anyone having to do with lessons garnered from experience have a theoretical connection with education. He points out that generally education is commonly and profitably viewed as having three loci: institution, product, and product. (36)   If this is the case, then Nietzsche clearly deserves to be considered a philosopher of education for one can find remarks in his writings on all of these points.   He was more than a dilletante when considering universities, their practices, and ideals.   More   importantly,   his   criticism of educational institutions and practices is deeply associated with his penetrating criticisms of Western philosophy. Yet this aspect of his thought has been consistently ignored. The above-mentioned encyclopedia, despite its comprehensive aim, contains but one single reference to Nietzsche, and this is merely remarks that one particular educator had read and been somewhat influenced by him. (37)

In a sense, the broad definition of education does make all thinkers involved with the theory of education. For example, one might claim that all philosophers, since they make claims about truth, must of necessity be concerned with the education of humanity inasmuch as they see the improvement, salvation, or morality of mankind tied to the acceptance of those truths. Plato was clearly concerned with education in this way. But one might claim that someone like Kant was concerned with education since he would have humanity accept the metaphysics and complementary ethics he described. While one might make this kind of claim and possibly many others like it, I would like to suggest that Nietzsche is paradigmatically concerned with education because of his life-centered philosophical method. His philosophical 'cause,' including method, aims, and style, is archetypically educative because it aims at nothing less than the transformation of the experiential quality of life.

My task of showing Nietzsche as educator is not one that can be demonstrated by easy, specific references to specific lines or even by novel interpretations of particularly arcane or little-known passages.   Rather I will attempt a substantive assessment of the meaning of Nietzsche's endeavors. What does it mean that he criticizes schools? What does it mean that he valued the contest? What does he mean with his image of the dance?

Answers to these questions reveal what education should mean.
Beyond that, it should never be forgotten that Nietzsche never
shyed away from identifying himself as a philosopher. And it is
here, in the role of philosopher that Nietzsche becomes an
educator. The tasks of philosopher and educator even conflate
into the human task: perpetual, striving self-enactment. Those
who most fully become what they are, then, are the most
philosophical and are therefore the best teachers of that most
important task.

The central role of meaning shapes Nietzsche's style. It
is important therefore to pay attention to style as an indicator
of intent. To my mind, one of the most striking features of
Nietzsche's style is its pre-emptory, didactic tone. Far from
being an academic, disinterested, professional philological or
philosophical discourse of proposals and criticisms, Nietzsche
deports himself as a vehement sage, and Zarathustra exemplifies
this tone, this style. Others have drawn attention to this.
Alderman rightly points out that Zarathustra comes to us as a
teacher and the lesson he teaches is the gift he brings:
"Zarathustra will teach us to become human." (38) In fact, I
would add by way of confirmation, the first words Zarathustra
speaks to those assembled in the marketplace are "I teach" (Ich
lehre). By looking at and interpreting Nietzsche as educator we
can learn what, for him, it means to be a philosopher. In the
first instance, the true philosopher will recognize, as did
Zarathustra, that preparation in philosophy does not mean
preparation for examinations. (The case of Zarathustra as
philosopher is considered in detail in the third chapter.) Not
linguistics, not history but life is the realm of the philosopher.

In Schopenhauer as Educator, Nietzsche understands the
meaning of the philosopher-as-educator as the person who confronts
the current pessimistic philosophy, who puts an end to the state
of disintegrating culture. (SE, 35) In the course of this
reflection on the task of the philosopher, Nietzsche (as he does
through the rest of his work) rejects 'naturalized' university
philosophy which makes the scholar the highest form of
philosopher. The criticism he makes about philosophy being
enslaved by the universities shows his basic disagreement with
understanding philosophy as merely rational analysis of the world.
He says: "And I consider useless every written word behind which
no challenge to action stands." (SE, 94) The character of
university philosophy does not demand transformation of one's
life, but only analysis and systematization. This insistence by
Nietzsche that philosophy mean something not only at the level of
intellect but also mean something at the level of lived life can
be seen in this paradigmatic assertion:

The only criticism of a philosophy which
is possible, and which also proves something—

20

that of seeing if one can live by it—has
never been taught at the universities: but
always criticism of words by words. (SE, 99)

That is to say that philosophy, and by inference all educational
institutions, ought to be concerned with the construction of
meaningful life possibilities. That university philosophers do
not challenge, do not measure the value of their values, do not
subject their truths to examination for their meaning for life are
all objections against the character of Western philosophy, both
in it professed ideal of metaphysics and its professed and actual
scholarly values. The task of considering Schopenhauer as
educator, the enterprise in the course of which Nietzsche makes
the above remark, is to show "how a new sphere of duties is to be
gained from this ideal and how one can obtain such a lofty goal
through regular activity, in short, to prove that this ideal
educates. (SE, 99) Schopenhauer, a philosopher ignored by
historians and philosophers of education, is considered by
Nietzsche as an educator because of his proposed ideal of man and
the implications of that ideal for life. If is probably fair to
say, too, that Nietzsche thought of Schopenhauer as this ideal
when he wrote this Untimely Meditation. If philosophy is to be
learned and measured by the innermost recesses of one's soul (SE,
24), if Nietzsche's intent is to "raise knowledge to the mightiest
effect" (NUL, 83), then philosophy must not only analyze the
existential exigencies of man but must provide lived, educating
solutions which justify human existence as the literal meaning of
the earth. Even if Nietzsche did reject Schopenhauer later on, I
still think the remarks on philosophy could have been written by
Nietzsche at virtually any point. That is to say that I do not
think Nietzsche ever abandoned the kind of philosophical task he
ascribed to Schopenhauer.

In Beyond Good and Evil, Nietzsche remarks how the Stoics
took existence only in their own image. He does so in the context
of objecting to any pretense that laws are "read off" from the
order of nature. But, he maintains, the position of the Stoics is
not at all unusual:

But this is an ancient, eternal story.
What formerly happened with the Stoics
still happens today, too, as soon as any
philosophy begins to believe in itself.
It always creates the world in its own
image; it cannot do otherwise. Philosophy
is this tyrannical drive itself, the most
spiritual will to power, to the 'creation of
the world,' to the causa prima. (BGE, 16)

Here Nietzsche holds that the world exists only as it has been
shaped by philosophical interpretations. Certainly this is a

21

radical departure from Western attempts to determine the character of the world independent of human knowing. But just as certainly, Nietzsche intends that philosophy should create the world, that the word exists only insofar as man has imposed his particular meanings onto it. The task of philosophy also has an artistic dimension, then, in the depictive reality of the world and the creation of modes of human conduct.

One sees in this conception of philosophy a remarkable identity with Nietzsche's conception of art. In Twilight of the Idols, he says of the artist's state of frenzy or intoxication that:

> In this condition one enriches everything out
> of one's own abundance: what one sees, what
> one desires, one sees swollen, pressing, strong,
> overladen with energy. The man in this
> condition transforms things until they mirror
> his power—until they are reflections of his
> perfection. This compulsion to transform
> into the perfect is—art. (TI, 72)

It would appear that the task of philosophy and art meet in the generation of the world in the self-image of man. Not surprisingly, Nietzsche claims that "Education is a continuation of procreation, and very often a kind of supplementary varnishing of it." (D, 299) As in so many other cases, Nietzsche denies the legitimacy of drawing ultimate distinctions between categories of human activity. Here, philosophy, art, and education meet in one, in a creation of the world, a creation which is to be understood as the meaningful transformation or metaphysical procreation of human life.

In Beyond Good and Evil, Nietzsche makes a number of remarks on the character of philosophy which all corroborate the claim that a primary concern of the philosopher is creation. Furthermore, creation in the realm of lived experience is the philosopher's particular responsibility since it is the meaning of the earth. That is to say that without the philosophical life, as the mode of human life which generates meaning, then indeed the lot of mankind would be meaningless. Nietzsche's criticisms of philosophers are to be understood in terms of his claim that the basic activity of philosophy is a creative one. Nietzsche rejects the notion that philosophy 'discovers' truths: "I have set up the most difficult idea of the philosopher. Learning is not enough! The scholar is the herd animal in the realm of knowledge—who inquires because he is ordered to and because others have done so before him.—" (WP, 421; cf WP, 422) Learning is not enough because living is the test of the philosopher's value. The philosopher is, in effect, the legislator and educator of human meaning. Nietzsche says:

> The philosopher as we understand him, we
> free spirits—as the man of the most
> comprehensive responsibility who has the
> conscience for the over-all development of
> man—this philosopher will make use
> of religions for his project of cultivation
> and education, just as he will make use of
> whatever political and economic states
> are at hand. (BGE, 72)

Just as Nietzsche argues for the use of religions here by the philosopher, so to the philosopher will use metaphysics and other philosophical activities as a means to an end. That they are necessary is not denied; Nietzsche freely admits their indispensability. Nevertheless, once positing creativity as the highest human/philosophical task, Nietzsche cannot insist on the value of anything except insofar as it is instrumental to that end. Thus, he objects to the taking of religions as absolute givens, as absolute truths:

> In the end, to be sure—to present the
> other side of the account of these
> religions, too, and to expose their
> uncanny dangerousness—one always pays
> dearly and terribly when religions do
> not want to be a means of education and
> cultivation in the philosopher's hand
> but insist on having their own sovereign
> way, when they themselves want to be
> ultimate ends and not means among other
> means. (BGE, 74)

Nietzsche does not object to the use of religion per se (and for that matter does not object to the invention of gods) (TSZ, 586), but does object to finding in any human creation the reason for the end of creation.

As is well known, Nietzsche is often inexorably strident in his denunciations of past values and philosophical interpretations of the world. He finds that philosophy as currently conceived and practised is either guilty of some limiting partialism or is wrongly grounded. In his notes, Nietzsche objected to Kant, claiming that Kant conceived philosophy merely as the science of the limitation of reason. (WP, 448) In another note he remarks on the Epicurean rejection of Aristotle's conception of philosophy, lauding their ability to distinguish between the art of discovering truth and the art of living:

> Philosophy as the art of discovering truth:

23

according to Aristotle. Contradicted by the
Epicureans, who made use of Aristotle's
sensualistic theory of knowledge: they
rejected the search for truth with irony:
'Philosophy as an art of living.' (WP, 449)

The task of the philosophers of the future, then, will be to
surpass any decadent valuations and in their stead teach man to
create new valuations, which is another way of saying new meanings
for human life. Such new philosophers will be responsible:

To teach man the future of man as his will,
as dependent on a human will, and to prepare
great ventures and over-all attempts to
discipline and cultivation by way of putting
an end to that gruesome dominion of nonsense
and accident that has so far been called
'history'--the nonsense of the 'greatest number'
is merely its ultimate form: at some time
new types of philosophers and commanders will
be necessary for that, and whatever has
existed on earth of concealed, terrible,
and benevolent spirits, will look pale
and dwarfed by comparison. (BGE, 117)

To the extent that it is possible, philosophers will dictate the
meaning and interpretation of the earth. The world will be what
man determines himself to be, since he is the being capable of
determining what his life means.

In a remarkable statement on the legislative character of
philosophers, Nietzsche says:

Genuine philosophers, however, are
commanders and legislators: they say
'thus it shall be.' They first determine
the Wither and For What of man, and in so
doing have at their disposal the preliminary
labor of all philosophical laborers, all who
have overcome the past. With a creative hand
they reach for the future, and all that is
and has been becomes a means for them, an
instrument, a hammer. Their 'knowing' is
creating, their creating is a legislation,
their will to to truth--is will to
power. (BGE, 136)

Ultimately, then, the world is nothing more than the system by
which one evaluates and determines meanings, for as is well known,
Nietzsche often proclaimed that there is no truth (which is to say
that there is no fixed meaning). Consequently, Nietzsche would

24

ask philosophers to generate those characterizations of the world which are most conducive to the future creation of human meaning.

In an abandoned attempt from 1872, "The Philosopher; Reflections on the Struggle Between Art and Knowledge," Nietzsche insists on the creative character of philosophy thus:

> I mean, philosophy does not follow the course
> of the other sciences, even if certain of the
> philosopher's territories gradually fall into
> the hands of science. Heraclitus can never be
> obsolete. Philosophy is invention beyond the
> limits of experience; it is the continuation
> of the mythical drive. It is thus
> essentially pictorial. (PT, 19)

Further, Nietzsche remarks on the metamorphosis of the world into a mirror of man himself, this recalling the definition of art above.

> What the philosopher is seeking is not
> truth, but rather the metamorphosis of
> the world into men. He strives for an
> understanding of the world with self-
> consciousness. He strives for an
> assimilation. He is satisfied when he
> has explained something anthropomorphically.
> Just as the astrologer regards the world as
> serving the single individual, the
> philosopher regards the world as a human
> being. (PT, 52)

In another of his notes, Nietzsche remarks quite consistently with his published remarks on the same topic that: "One seeks a picture of the world in that philosophy in which we feel freest; i.e., in which our most powerful drives feels free to function. This will also be the case with me." (WP, 418) If the world, then, is the product of particular depictions reflecting the character and meaning of man himself, all individuals will not choose the same depictions since not all men have the same character. They exist at different levels of power. "Learning changes us... But at the bottom of us, really 'deep down,' there is, of course, something unteachable, some granite of spiritual fatum, of predetermined decision and answer to predetermined selected questions." (BGE, 162) Furthermore, and this is crucial, one can only ask about truth or falsity of the depiction in reference to another frame of reference, namely to another depiction. Thus is to be understood Nietzsche's genealogical evaluation of other systems of philosophy and religions. He does not measure them against an idealist conception of truth, but against the depiction of will to power as the highest criterion of judgment on all matters, a criterion he has declared to be true. He thinks, of course, that this interpretation allows the experience of the greatest freedom even if it does strip away all the former conditions of human security and well-being, god, eternal truth, reason and the like.

Nietzsche would challenge philosophy, then, to render depictions according to which man could live most meaningfully and express the greatest interpretive creativity. This, of course, requires moving beyond traditional structures of meaning. These structures of meaning were by no means completely unnecessary to be sure. Priding himself on his historical sense in philosophy, Nietzsche knew that these moral systems of the past/present were necessary stages in the development of man. Having once been adopted as expedients meant that they had at that time been adopted as necessary. In fact, they form the basis of the possibility of any further interpretation. It was necessary that these structures of meaning, these philosophical and religious systems were played out, that man lived them in order to test their truth value, their value for life. Kaufmann perceptively notes: "The different philosophical systems are to be considered as educative methods of the spirit: they have always developed one particular force of the spirit best by their one-sided demand to see things just so and not otherwise." (39) How caustic he became towards these value structures as obstacles to adopting a metaphysics of creativity, it is to be kept in mind that they were necessary phase, skins to be shed, but skins that were once useful. Indeed, the possibility of Nietzsche's conclusions ever having arisen is contingent upon these value structures having played themselves out, having lived beyond their usefulness. They pose the greatest obstacles in that rather than recognizing them for what they are, historical stages and temporal expedients, philosophers and nations have transformed them into timeless truths, into unquestioned conditions of life. Whereas Nietzsche calls them 'idols,' the world calls them 'truths.' The true philosopher, as a creative individual, denies them in order to surpass them. Such a task is indicated by Nietzsche in Ecce Homo, in which he speaks thus of philosophy:

> Philosophy, as I have so far understood and
> lived it, means living voluntarily among
> ice and high mountains—seeking out every-
> thing strange and questionable in
> existence, everything so far placed under a
> ban of morality. Long experience, acquired
> in the course of such wanderings in what
> is forbidden, taught me to regard
> the causes that have so far prompted
> moralizing and idealizing in a very different
> light from what may seem desirable: the
> hidden history of the philosophers, the
> psychology of the great names, came to light

for me. (EH, 218)

To borrow Sartre's characterization of Baudelaire, Nietzsche retreated into a solitude where living and invention are identical. (40) The philosopher is the educator of humanity in his dictating terms of meaning by which to evaluate through actual life the world itself. Nietzsche evaluates the competing systems genealogically, i.e., by looking at them as expedients, looking to see under what conditions one would have adopted such and such 'truths.' In this way he is not necessarily making any metaphysical statements about the world in itself; neither does he even need a world. He means his life and works as a reflection of his power, depicting the world and life as so much possibility awaiting the creative hand of the philosopher. The denial of past systems of 'truth' is a condition for the possibility of creativity. Thus the philosopher, far from being a rational propounder of the nature of the true, is a "terrible explosive endangering everything." (EH, 281)

Thus far I have stressed that commentators have focussed primarily on the metaphysical claims of Nietzsche and have engaged him on the grounds of assessing such claims. In so doing I think these philosophers have de-emphasized the portion of Nietzsche's intent that requires not mere intellectual response but the response of a person's whole life. The intent of Nietzschean philosophy is not assent or disagreement with bookish arguments but engaging one at the level of meaning-constitution, at which will, action and identity become constitutive of one another. Thus far, no philosopher has with his or her life offered a refutation or confirmation of, for example, Nietzsche's notion of the will to power. Yet articles, books, and doctoral dissertations about on the subject. Yet it seems to me that Nietzsche demands such lived interpretation, because the very meaning and fulfillment of philosophy is in the realm of human self enactment. And in this philosophical self-enactment it becomes clear that Nietzsche is an educator. More properly, one might say that philosophy and education are two sides of a coin. Philosophy means educative enterprise in the widest sense. Kaufmann is surely right, then, when he echoes Nietzsche that Nietzsche's reflections on Schopenhauer as Educator are really reflections on Nietzsche as Educator. (41)

Nietzsche asked of Schopenhauer what ideal he created for man. If we ask that selfsame question of Nietzsche, we might answer that the ideal he set above man was simply to be man. Yet there is perhaps no higher goal, no ideal that we can learn more from than the truly human problem of generating meaning for life. This generation of meaning in life is truly a creative task, for we must bring it out of the nothing of an inherently meaningless

27

universe.

In the following chapters, the particulars of the move towards meaningful philosophical education, towards human self-enactment will be surveyed. In Chapter 2, a review of Nietzsche's critique of the formal educational institution is offered. In Chapter 3, his insistence on the agon as the educational process will be examined. Chapter 4 looks at the notion of lie and/or mask which is one of the most important kinds of contest that Nietzsche urges. Chapter 5 examines the proposed product of education, the dance of man.

Chapter 2

NIETZSCHE ON UNIVERSITY EDUCATION

> Once and for all, there is
> a great deal I do not want
> to know.—Wisdom sets bounds
> even to knowledge.
>
> Nietzsche
> (TI, 23)

That Nietzsche intimately links philosophy and education is seen
further in a consideration of the many and vitriolic remarks he
makes on contemporary university education. He objects to the
current practices as well as the professed ideals of the schools
he knew intimately. Though he never gives as explicitly sustained
an effort in consideration of educational theory as he did to
other of his concerns, he certainly makes a great number of
remarks about education. While at Basel he gave a series of five
lectures (though he originally intended more) on The Future of Our
Educational Institutions. It was in these lectures that he
first publicly outlines what he takes to be the serious
shortcomings of university education. While he never chose to
publish these earliest pronouncements of his dissatisfaction,
Nietzsche never stopped denouncing decadence perpetrated in the
name of education.

By following out Nietzsche's criticisms of the practices
of education, one sees as well his criticism of the current state
of philosophy. Looking at the many problems of education through
the eyes and ideals of Schopenhauer at first, Nietzsche criticizes
the practices of scholarship, the control of the universities by
ideologies of statism and science, the democratization of the
universities, and the moral vision founding and informing
educational theory and practice. Nietzsche's radical
aristocratism, his vision of man as led by and justified by the
highest types, engenders further criticism of the lack of solitude
in the university, of the idea that philosophy consists
essentially in criticism, domination of the universities by
idealist metaphysics, in short of of the obstacles universities
pose for the higher type. These criticisms span the breadth of
Nietzsche's corpus and no single text can be said to contain them
all. And if the written portion of his criticism were not enough,
Nietzsche's biography reveals that he grappled with these problems
not only at the intellectual level but also in his personal life.

In his essay on Schopenhauer, Nietzsche ponders an apparent opposition of two maxims about education. One of these stresses education cultivating the real strength or ability of an individual, to the exclusion of all other, lesser talents. The other holds that education ought to cultivate all abilities in an individual, perhaps to the exclusion of any single dominant talent (SE, 8). He decides, however, that the opposition is merely apparent:

> Perhaps, then these two maxims are in no
> way opposite? Perhaps the one says that
> man shall have a center, the other that
> he shall also have a periphery. (SE, 8)

The 'contradiction' is only apparent because the aim of education is the whole person, not particular talents or strengths. It is one of Nietzsche's primary tacts in the assessment of current education that because of its practices, its submission to scholarly and scientific ideals, education develops one aspect of an individual's abilities to the exclusion of others. In short, education produces 'inverse cripples,' the kinds of creatures Zarathustra encounters at one point (TSZ, 249-254).

Contrary to what one might expect from a professor in a highly specialized academic field, Nietzsche made scholarship one of his primary targets throughout his criticism of education. And much of his criticism centers around the inverse crippling of scholars. It should be remembered that Nietzsche made his formal appearance in the world of academia with a book that contained no footnotes, this suggesting to the world of German scholasticism a superficial and insignificant book. His disdain for scholarship found clear articulation not longer after the Birth of Tragedy in Schopenhauer as Educator:

> Scholarship has the same relationship to
> wisdom as righteousness has to holiness:
> It is cold and dry, it is loveless and knows
> no deep feelings of inadequacy or longing.
> It is as useful to itself as it is harmful
> to its servants, insofar as it transmits
> its own character to the latter, thereby
> ossifying their humanity. (SE, 71)

Since the pursuit of scholarship patterns the character of the life of those who follow its path, Nietzsche objects to its minimal creativity. Once identifying humans as essentially creative, Nietzsche must repudiate any kind of 'system' that defines human goals and ideals completely beforehand. By adopting the idea of scholarship, one adopts a structure of meaning and values that is dictated by prior generations of scholars. Having knowledge as its ideal, scholarship might seem in a position to advance the cause of human creativity. But the kind of truth that scholarship reveals and the use to which scholarship is put, constrain the liberating capacity of truth. Scholarship puts up a kind of smokescreen in front of the great books, the great minds:

> Let us have as few people as possible between the productive minds and the hungry recipient minds! The middlemen almost unconsciously adulterate the food which they supply. For their work as middlemen they want too high a fee for themselves, and this is drawn from the original, productive spirits—namely interest, admiration, leisure, money, and other advantages. — Accordingly, we should always look upon the teacher as a necessary evil. (HATH, II, 335)

In his essay on Schopenhauer, Nietzsche remarked that scholars can be motivated by (a) compulsion to contradict, (b) poverty and dryness of feeling, (c) little self-esteem; modesty that crawls and does not fly, (d) a mere habit of collecting, and (e) a flight from boredom (SE, 72-77).

So motivated, the scholar is in an unlikely position to meet the criteria of a genuine philosopher, a genuine teacher. The teacher/scholar is a caricature of a philosopher, even of a human being, for his personality has become so peculiarly developed, and he is guided by less than noble motives. To be sure, Nietzsche did not feel this way about all scholars; there were some exceptions within his personal circle of acquaintances. But by and large, this was surely his opinion: the scholar could not be an effective teacher because he did not possess the requisites to become a philosopher. Nietzsche puts Kant in this category:

> A scholar can never become a philosopher; even Kant could not do this and remained to the end, in spite of the inborn drive of his genius, in a state of pupation. Whoever thinks that I am doing Kant an injustice with these words does not know what a true philosopher is; namely, not only a great thinker but also a true man; and when has a true man ever come from a scholar? (SE, 189)

Such harsh criticism (so early, too, in his publishings) indicates that Nietzsche could not equate the academic, philosophical scholar with the genuine philosopher. Nietzsche became ever more derogatory towards Kant, who clearly has had a powerful impact as a philosopher. He despised the kind of professorial philosophy that Kant represented (though as with everything else, Nietzsche did not categorically reject Kant), the intensely abstract speculation that was apparently divorced from all lived experience.

Nietzsche thought that by adopting an academic position as a scholar, one let books stand in the way of experiencing the fullness, vitality, and even misery of life. The scholar becomes a kind of slave to intellectual fashion. He merely reacts to the books and articles that happen his way. He is not procreative: "Scholars spend all of their energies on saying Yes and No, on criticism of what others have thought – they themselves no longer think." (EH, 253) Indeed, the self-subjugation of the scholar to the world of university regulation may itself be indicative of a lack of creative potential. For the most part, Nietzsche thinks that the scholar is the herd animal in the academic world. (WP, 421; WP, 422) Insofar as the scholar appropriates the intellectual mores of his discipline, the regulation of the university and the moral dictates of its philosophy of education, he is bound, even confined within a situation not of his own making. In a word, the scholar cannot be a philosopher because he is not independent enough to give an example in thinking and living. According to the image Nietzsche presents, scholars claim as their domain an unpretentious and unthreatening truth, from which nothing is to be feared. Theirs is a complacent truth which does not challenge:

> What is wrong with sending scholars into
> new and dangerous hunting grounds, where
> courage, sense, and subtlety in every way
> are required, is that they cease to be of
> any use precisely where the 'great hunt,'
> but also the great danger, begins: precisely
> there they lose their keen eye and nose.
> (BGE, 59)

They even lust after the honor of the masses in order to validate themselves, an act which Nietzsche could never forgive, for in addition to thus being guilty of a kind of intellectual heteronomy, it would also be the lowest conceivable type of heteronomy, involving as it does the masses (WP, 792).

Consistently, some of Nietzsche's most vicious prose was spent excoriating scholars. For all that, one can find some remarks which praise the value of the struggle necessary to become a scholar. In other words, though the ideal may be ultimately decadent, still it is not an easy ideal to achieve, and Nietzsche admires the strength of the asceticism which is involved in scholarship, for such asceticism indicates a mastery at least of one's own being (though not a mastery entirely in keeping with what Nietzsche would want ultimately). Kaufman rightly points out that Nietzsche's ethical doctrine revolves around this conception of self-overcoming. Nietzsche admire the scholar to the extent that he has done precisely this, overcome himself, structured his lived reality in a way that is liberated from venal and common value hierarchy.

Yet such asceticism is not an end in itself. Rather, the asceticism that Nietzsche praises is lived as a tool in the service of higher life. Nietzsche, as indicated, thought that scholars could be motivated by any number of low and base considerations. However, at least in some cases, it seems that the scholar's life can be motivated by an unlikely drive: justice. (SE, 77) When the asceticism of the scholar works in service of a higher ideal, a higher form of humanity, then, it can be the case that the scholar functions in elevating life. Nietzsche's former teacher, Corsen for example, he exempted from his criticism for that one remained a natural enemy of philistinism while at the same time remaining a most rigorous scholar. (SLFN, 45) Jacob Burckhardt, too, Nietzsche held always in high esteem. In these individuals scholarly asceticism is proof of their endurance.

And yet, in the end, such endurance must always be turned to creative activity. This can be seen in Nietzsche's remarks on why it is desirable to pursue a scientific education for a time:

> The value of strictly pursuing science for
> a time does not lie precisely in the results,
> for these, in proportion to the ocean of what
> is worth knowing, are but an infinitesmally
> small drop. But it gives an additional
> energy, decisiveness, and a toughness of
> endurance; it teaches how to attain an aim
> suitably. In so far it is very valuable,
> with a view to all that is done later, once,
> to have been a scientific man. (HATH, I, 236)

The scholarly/scientific rigor that is exacted in the university can be turned to a positive good, but only if the period of asceticism is turned to a creative response to living. Nietzsche himself remarks that though his own personal stage of scholarliness was ultimately only an intermediary stage, still it was necessary. (EH, 282) The pitfall of scholarly asceticism is this: "In every ascetic morality man worships one part of himself as a God, and is obliged, therefore to diabolise the other parts." (HATH, I, 140) And Nietzsche finds that such a diabolization stunts the development of the wholly creative individual. But, to reiterate the point made just above and to expand it to the whole of the history of the educational process, such stages of

33

asceticism/scholarship are necessary for the lessons they do
impart; they are the conditions of the possibility, to put it in
Kantian phraseology, for the liberation from those stages. The
scholarship of the universities may have been an accomplishment in
knowledge at one historical stage and may always be so in some
way. But that stage cannot produce the creativity which
Nietzsche's vision of truth as interpretation demands. To make
one further observation, one might say that ascetic practices
engender control and mastery (and their concomitant virtues in
scholarship), but Nietzsche does not think that these virtues can
of themselves engender, the creativity he sees as metaphysically
desirable.

Related to his criticism of scholarship as devitalizing
education is Nietzsche's criticism of the increasing
democratization of education. In The Future of our Educational
Institutions, Nietzsche says that just as the masses must serve
the geniuses of culture, so, too, must education serve the
interests of the highest types. Because Nietzsche's philosophical
anthropology rests on radical aristocratism, his position on
education cannot be other than it is. Since he locates meaning
only in the highest types of human beings, the democratization of
education ruins the prospect of diverting time and energy on the
part of the culture as well as the educators, towards these
highest types. Just as Nietzsche maintains that mankind finds its
value in working on behalf of the noble types so too must
education eschew democratic trends. He therefore resists
democratic education since it is:

> essentially the means of ruining exceptions
> for the good of the rule. Higher education:
> essentially the means of directing taste
> against the exceptions for the good of the
> mediocre. (WP, 933)

While Nietzsche's response to the democratization of the
universities is one of rejection and dismissal, the needs of any
civilization require some form of common education at all social
levels. Nietzsche could not object to the education of
individuals in accordance with the needs of a civilization. He
does, however, think that the needs of education require an
aristocratic pursuit in order to advance the highest types of
human beings. Nietzsche likens the education of a superior type
to attending to a pregnancy, having to respond to all its strange
appetites. (HATH, II, 140) Genuine educators must even make
themselves nurses of remarkable invalids. In the end, the formal
profession of education must be entirely on behalf of the superior
types. Nietzsche says:

> All higher education belongs to the exceptional
> alone: one must be privileged to have a right

34

> to so high a privilege. Great and fine things
> can never be common property: <u>pulchrum</u> <u>est</u>
> <u>paucorum</u> <u>hominum</u>. What is the <u>cause</u> of
> the decline of German culture? that 'higher
> education' is no longer a privilege - . (TI, 64)

Conceived as instruments of cultural inculcation, German universities fail because they do not direct themselves to those capable of receiving and generating culture. The masses, by definition, are undistinguished and undistinguishable, and any attempt to cultivate them must end in the weakening of the universities.

In <u>The Revolt of the Masses</u>, Ortega y Gassett gives a stern, Nietzsche-inspired analysis of he detrimental demands of science and the state on the possibility of education. I mention this book because it seems to me to be a fully-stated, logical conclusion of Nietzsche's argument. Following Nietzsche, he argues that the advance of science is followed by an increasing specialization on the part of its practitioners. Nietzsche referred to this as a weakening of education (FEI, 36), since in order to fit the needs of science or of the state, persons had to compromise certain of their abilities in order to devote themselves more fully to one aspect. Such a state of affairs is destructive of the possibility of thorough-going independence. Subscription to a machinery of education in the service of an ideology seeking its own partisans and workers stands in opposition to Nietzsche's creative, autonomous ideal. Machinery contributes to anonymity, in products as well as in self-identification.

> Machinery is impersonal; it robs the piece
> of work of its pride, of the individual
> merits and defects that cling to all work
> that is not machine-made - in other words,
> of its bit of humanity. Formerly, all
> buying from handicraftsmen meant a mark of
> distinction for their personalities, with
> whose productions people surround themselves.
> (HATH, II, 342)

If education is conceived of as an ideological machine in the service of some state or science, then the result is that any attempt to climb higher, to improve or even overthrow that ideology, to becoming artistic, to becoming philosophical must of necessity involve great effort. For if, as Nietzsche says, the point of higher education is to turn man into a machine, then that could only mean that education seeks to socialize individuals in such a way that <u>they</u> <u>do</u> <u>not</u> <u>find</u> themselves limited or oppressed by the prevailing ideology; quite the contrary, they will find in it their <u>meaning</u>, and this as the result of the philosophical

35

endeavor that constitutes the human act.

Professor Nietzsche's criticism is thorough-going, and he spares the university almost never. One might imagine that this is quite remarkable since most of the years of his life involved schools in one way or another. It is not too much to say that Nietzsche saw the schools as the point of transference between society and persons. Where society failed man philosophically so too it must fail him educationally. Nietzsche's criticisms of philosophy and education coincide in their indictment of a lack of an emancipating vision of man.

One can wonder why Nietzsche chose to concern himself with the question of education through an examination of Schopenhauer. After all, one can make the same criticisms of scholarly life without having to refer to Schopenhauer. To be sure, in many ways Nietzsche's book about Schopenhauer is mostly about Nietzsche himself rather than the philosopher mentioned in the title. But as Sartre said of Baudelaire one can equally well maintain of Nietzsche's relation with the entire world:

> Objects were pretexts, reflections, screens
> but they were never of any value in them-
> selves; their only purpose was to give him
> an opportunity of contemplating himself while
> he was looking at them. (1)

Indeed, Nietzsche realized this later on with respect to his own relationship with Schopenhauer. But beyond this insight, Nietzsche himself makes clear why he concerns himself with Schopenhauer, a philosopher only rarely mentioned in histories of educational theory at all, and never as an educator. He does so because first and foremost Schopenhauer is a philosopher who gives (Nietzsche at that time thought) new direction to the possibilities of life. Schopenhauer earns his credentials as an educator insofar as he provides a new example for man to live by. He does not propose a scholarly ideal. Neither does he concern himself particularly with academics. Nietzsche credits Schopenhauer as an educator because he gives an example of how to live.

In his judgment on the value of a philosopher, Nietzsche makes it eminently clear that philosophy implies a concern with education, not by books or words, but by one's actual lived example. He says:

> I judge a philosopher by whether he is able
> to serve as an example. There is no doubt
> that through his example he can draw whole
> nations after him; Indian history, which
> is almost the history of Indian philosophy,

36

> proves this. But the example must be given
> through visible life and not merely through
> books, that is, as the Greek philosophers
> taught, through one's expressions, attitudes
> clothing, food and way of life rather than
> through speaking, and least of all through
> writing. (SE, 18)

The example of the philosopher as educator cannot be identical with that of the philosopher as scholar for the latter ideal stands in opposition to creative example of how to live. The example of scholar has been lived and, so, tested. Its limits have been seen.

In examining a philosopher for his educational import, one attempts to determine the sphere of duties that follows from his ideal. That is to say, one looks to see what lived differences that ideal would make. Contrary to the ideals of scholarship, Nietzsche thinks that the duties of the Schopenhauerian education would be "to further the production of the philosopher, of the artist and of the saint within us and outside us, and thereby to work at the consummation of nature." (SE, 56) This last clause indicates that Nietzsche is still under the spell of purposeful cosmology, purpose that man must work with in order to perfect. Although he would come to abandon any kind of intentionality behind nature, Nietzsche will continue to insist that the philosophical ideal places demands of the most far-reaching kind on an individual or society. To educate means to culture, and culture "demands from him [the student] not only inner experience, not only the judgment of the exterior world of flux, but finally, and chiefly, action." (SE, 62) Such an ideal demands the renunciation of the sedate, scholarly ideal. Nietzsche's ethical directive of amor fati does not justify a quietistic mode of life. One must create to the extent that one can, the meaning of life. Philosophers serve as educators in that they serve as examples. Not all individuals, of course, can be as independent as Nietzsche's Ubermensch ideal. But one ought to be, because one is human, creative. The doctrine of amor fati means nothing more than this: to become what one is, to be human, to value the human, to signify the human.

Nietzsche thought Schopenhauer had liberated humanity from some of the traditional categories which bound creativity. Nietzsche claimed Schopenhauer apparently aligned his ideal of mankind with the perfection of nature. But even so, the ideal of mankind was not a mere given of nature, but one in which man has a hand: "Even in the case of the greatest man, his own ideal stands far above him." (SE,23) The responsibility of the philosopher as educator, Nietzsche says, is to disclose the meaning of being human through lived example. Such example discloses that one's true being "does not lie hidden deep inside you but immeasurably high above you." (SE, 5) The task of education is liberation, liberation to move towards that which stands far above one. Becoming what one is, then, is a matter of determining one's possibilities, the meaning of ones possibilities, and the attempt to live the most noble of those options. The philosopher is the individual who says, in effect: "this is the picture of life as a whole...learn from it the meaning of your life." (SE, 26) The philosopher is the creative educator who opens new meanings for the possibilities of life.

Nietzsche thought that in the main, universities gave poor examples of living for meaning, living for creativity. One of their chief defects is impeding solitude (solitude understood as apartness from existing intellectual, aesthetic, and moral givens):

> I have gradually seen the light as to the
> most universal deficiency in our kind of
> cultivation and education: no one learns,
> no one strives after, no one teaches —
> the endurance of solitude. (D, 188)

The virtue of solitude for Nietzsche was its capacity to engender reflectiveness. It is one thing to teach critical reflection about texts and aesthetic objects. It is another to teach critical reflection about human possibility. When solitude is abandoned, the mass or herd ideal takes its place. And if Nietzsche's criticisms of democratic life show anything, they show how the pursuit of individualism is rendered antithetical to the common ethic.

As will be seen in the following chapter, Nietzsche criticizes educational procedures for their insistence upon mass conformity and unanimity. He will criticize the dependence, in particular, of the student on the teacher. As an opposing ideal he holds that the philosopher/educator is an instrument whom the student must repudiate in order to achieve necessary independence and solitude. And, of course, as in all aspects of his thought, Nietzsche is a radical aristocrat who does not think that many will be capable of attaining such solitude or independence from the teacher. Nevertheless, such an argument does not undermine, eo ipso, the validity of the ideal for it remains an ideal even if no one could achieve practical identity with the theoretical demands. Consequently, he claims that contrary to the democratic practices of his time, great success belongs to the educator who does not seek to educate everyone, but only

> a single individual, and in doing so looks
> neither to the right nor the left. The
> previous century is superior to ours in
> precisely this, that it contained so many

> individually educated people, together with
> just as many individual educators who had
> here discovered the task of their life--
> and with their task also their dignity,
> in their own eyes and in those of all
> others of 'good society.' (D, 114-115)

Contrary to the practice of large universities with large faculties with large student bodies, Nietzsche holds as an ideal the relation that would obtain between a teacher and a small number of students. This, in fact, is the model of Zarathustra. Nietzsche's proclaimer of the overman does not choose the university as his podium because his doctrine of the overman requires solitude. Since Nietzsche would specify that solitude is a condition of genuine education, solitude that can be put to use as the ground of creativity, then the democratization of educational institutions must be a drawback to genuine education.

There are other criticisms in Nietzsche which are profitable to examine, both for their implications for education as well as for the reconstruction, as it were, of philosophy. The principle that guided criticism of the scholar, the lack of solitude, and increasing democratic society makes itself evident here again. Nietzsche opposed the following: (a) moral systems which attempt to impose an estimation of the value of life, (b) understanding philosophy as only a critical activity, and (c) philosophers who take idealist or realist metaphysics as their highest task. These approaches to philosophy, I would say, Nietzsche understood as embodiments of decadent moral choices. They seemed to him to embody destructive choices of man, closing off the world of man (beyond which there is merely insignificant existence). As elements of human education, they seem to minimize the meaning of man. My discussion of these three items is necessarily global. The important point is to see the thrust of his campaign against a morality of Procrustes.

In regards to the first item, Nietzsche holds that the value of life cannot be estimated because of its first principle, power. Thus Nietzsche says: "Judgments, value judgments concerning life, for or against, can in the last resort never be true: they possess value only as symptoms, they come into consideration only as systems." (TI, 30) In defining highest goods or a summum bonum, a moral system limits the possibility of creativity. The highest good is a symptom in Nietzsche's eyes for it reveals the particular expedient required by the person or the people who adopt that particular ideal.

The idea of moving beyond good and evil, for Nietzsche, implies moving beyond the limiting conditions of imposed moral valuations into the realm of new meaning and possibility. As an individual appropriates a particular moral system, he is in effect

39

limiting his own creativity, his own ability to be self-creative. One might say that "education into" a particular moral system is no education at all. Nietzsche identifies the idea of education with that of liberation, and he just as clearly takes the existence of moral systems as possibly entrapping. That is not to deny, as noted before, that education into a particular moral system, for an individual or for a culture, might constitute a necessary stage in development. It is merely to say that within a given system, one is working with pre-given limitations. If there is, after all, no truth, then it makes little sense to proceed according to one moral system as if it could contain all possible 'truth,' i.e., possible human interpretation of the world. In a simple way, this repudiation of education into particular moral systems, is derivative from Nietzsche's epistemological concerns: there is no truth, therefore there is no moral order independent of the of the moral order created by human valuing. Yet Nietzsche thought that in a more profound way it was moral considerations which spoke through professed philosophical systems. He is no exception to his own suspicion. It might even be claimed that Nietzsche's metaphysics derives from his morality: to advance the cause of human life, there is no truth; to expand the realm of human valuing, there is no truth. The repudiation of classical metaphysics and any moral order based on such a metaphysics, Nietzsche took to mean liberation from a necessary stage of development.

The task of philosophy is understood to be undergoing a transformation from understanding what is metaphysically given to creating what is morally desirable. Hence is to be understood the criticism that Nietzsche puts to the university order of education which is founded on and perpetuates the kind of inellectual task ordained by idealist metaphysics: creation, not mere interpretation of truth. The moral estimations of the past, Nietzsche claims "have hitherto most obstructed the course of philosophy." (WP, 413)

Philosophy as morally charged disallows a mere academic, a mere critical philosophy. The initial reasons for this will be evident from the argument of the first chapter which showed Nietzsche's mandating philosophy with existential responsibility, with the transformation of life by teaching. If universities, however, construe philosophy as the province of academics, they are failing quite seriously to return lived answers to the lived questions out of which philosophical activity springs. Criticism is not, however, without pertinent value. But philosophical criticism has value only as an instrument, it is not the whole of philosophy itself.

> I insist that people stop confounding
> philosophical laborers, and scientific
> men generally, with philosophers;

40

> precisely at this point we should be
> strict about giving 'each his due,' and
> not far too much to those and far too
> little to these.
>   It may be necessary for the education
> of a genuine philosopher that he himself
> has also once stood on all these steps
> on which his servants, the scientific
> laborers of philosophy, remain standing—
> have to remain standing. (BGE, 135)

Philosophy is not merely intellectual criticism whether of a dialectical or critical stripe. These activities can be instrumental and educative, but Nietzsche clearly indicates the aim of the philosopher's task: the creation of values. (BGE, 136) The best way to understand this statement of task, I think,is to understand Nietzsche as saying that creation of new ways of valuing is desirable. Nietzsche's writing may be understood as attempts at new ways of valuing life and existence. Philosophy must not remain immured at the level of rational criticism of the world.

With respect to Nietzsche's position on metaphysics, it has been argued all along that he attempts and would have others attempt new metaphysical interpretations of the world. However, his understanding of metaphysics is different from, say, an idealist position on the nature of the world. According to Nietzsche, nothing is. All that Nietzsche leaves to the idealist philosopher is the imaginary concept of being. (WP, 570)

Nietzsche's conception of the myth of being, developed primarily in the later writings (the Twilight of the Idols, for example) is important to consider, for traditionally, metaphysics is considered the pivotal concern of philosophy on which all the rest of its activities hinge. It is clear that by the end of his life Nietzsche rejected the intelligibility of the question of being as a question born of a false dichotomy between 'real' and 'apparent.' Nonetheless, it is equally clear that he did identify some features of existence in a manner that could only be called metaphysical (for he does identify first principles of human and worldly existence). What he rejects in the notion of 'being' is not metaphysical interpretive philosophy, but the particular answer given to the metaphysical question by idealists and realists alike. His vision of philosophy, therefore, did not have the rational apropriation of being at its center, for he considered such an enterprise as misguided ab initio. Consequently, too, any education which is structured around such a conception of philosophy will suffer as a result, being informed by that decadent and misleading notion.

These objections constitute the argument against both

41

current philosophy and educational practice. To judge from Nietzsche's depiction, there would seem to be only banality, sterility and decadence on a grand scale. But with the aplomb that is peculiar to Nietzsche he never despairs of the situation. Rather than abandon philosophy, he seeks its liberation, hoping to refound the principles of human education.

The hope he nourishes is hope fostered by confidence in the human (though not necessarily in any specific human). There are for Nietzsche men whose accomplishments function redemptively, that is to say, whose accomplishments hold back the shadows of meaninglessness however briefly. The nature of these accomplishments can, I believe, be seen through an examination of their agonal character, to which the next chapter is devoted.

Before closing this discussion, I think that a brief look at some moments of Nietzsche's biography show a parallel between his own experiences and the kind of emancipation he sought and thought he achieved for philosophy as a living discipline. All biographers of Nietzsche draw attention to the remarkable way in which he received his appointment to the university at Basel in February of 1869, being awarded his doctoral degree without having written a dissertation! Despite this appointment, which was a high accolade, he was not long in forming harsh opinions of the kind of education that prevailed there. The following comment was penned in 1873, only four years after his most extraordinary appointment.

> Symptoms of a decay of education are everywhere, a complete extirpation; haste, the subsiding waters of religion, national conflicts, science fragmenting and disintegrating, the contemptible cash and pleasure economy of the educated classes, their lack of love and grandeur. It is clearer and clearer to me that the learned classes are in every respect a part of this movement. They become more thoughtless and loveless with every day. Everything, art as well as science, serves the approaching barbarity. Where should we turn? The great deluge of barbarity is at the door: Since we really have nothing whatsoever with which to defend ourselves and are all a part of rhis movement. What is to be done? The attempt to warn the actually present powers, to join with them, and to subdue those strata from which the danger of barbarism threatens while there is still time. But every alliance with the 'educated' is to be rejected. This is the

> greatest enemy, for it hinders the physician
> and would disavow the disease. (PT, 102)

This is a remarkably bleak picture. The allegedly educated do not recognize the condition of their own barbarism! What is called for at the least is an overhaul of the major culture-bearing and culture-inculcating institutions of civilization, the schools.

One can find symptoms of Nietzsche's impatience with the universities even earlier than the above-quoted remark. In a letter of 15 December, 1870, less than two years after his appointment to Basel he wrote:

> At long last I too understand what
> Schopenhauer's reflections on academic
> wisdom are all about. A really radical
> living for truth just isn't possible in
> a university. Nothing revolutionary
> will ever come out of such a place.
> (NSP, 14)

In the letter, Nietzsche goes on to ask his correspondent, Erwin Rhode, if it is not possible to establish some kind of intellectual community apart from the maelstrom of the university in which truth could be pursued independent of the existing social institutions. This was a live aspiration of Nietzsche's for some time thought nothing ever came of it. But Nietzsche's disenchantment with the university did not necessarily develop after he began teaching. Indeed, the evening before he was to commence his new life as a professor, he wrote:

> The last moment has come, the last
> evening I shall spend in my old home;
> tomorrow morning I go out into the wide,
> wide world, into a new, unfamiliar
> profession, into a heavy and oppressive
> atmosphere of duty and work. (SLFN, 43)

Having such an ominous presage of what university life, from the professor's point of view, would be like, it is no wonder that Nietzsche could not long bear its atmosphere. One wonders whether he would have been able to stay in the university much longer had his health held out. But, like Zarathustra from the house of the scholars, he did leave, and left banging the doors behind him.

Apart from his recurrent and disabling illnesses, Nietzsche's leaving the university could very well be interpreted as being the logical outcome of living his own judgments on the place. Now, Nietzsche could not just strictly engage in criticism of the university practices per se, such as criticism of teaching

43

methods or curriculum or the like, for it was the grounding ideology that he took exception to. Thus, when Nietzsche criticizes educational theory, he is ultimately engaging in philosophical criticism, since the universities in their ideals and practices reflect their grounding philosophy. In his book on Schopenhauer, Nietzsche had advocated moving philosophy as a discipline or an activity outside the university altogether. Thus, the philosopher would not be bound to serve or live under a community or university ideology. Nietzsche in essence wanted to put philosophy outside the control of the prevailing ideology, and give it a freedom which pertains to the very nature of philosophy:

> For this reason it seems most important
> to me that there be a higher tribunal,
> outside the universities, to supervise
> and judge these institutions in respect
> to culture which they promote; and as soon
> as philosophy withdraws from the universities
> and cleanses itself of all unworthy
> considerations and obscurities, it will
> necessarily become such a tribunal.
> (SE, 107)

Though he does criticize the practices of scholars and the academic division of labor of universities, Nietzsche must ultimately grapple with the ideology grounding the universities. Nietzsche considered himself less and less a philologist and more and more a philosopher the more he engaged in that kind of evaluation. For that reason, too, he considered himself more a teacher, once outside the university. In a letter to Rhode, part of which is cited above, he cites the benefits of liberation from the university, benefits which he would in fact experience:

> Afterward we can become real teachers
> by levering ourselves with all possible
> means out of the atmosphere of these
> things and by becoming not only wiser but
> also better human beings. Here too I
> feel the need to be true. And that is
> another reason why I cannot go on
> breathing the academic atmosphere much
> longer. (SLFN, 74)

Indeed, in the following month, in January of 1871, having been at Basel less than two years, Nietzsche applied for a vacant chair in philosophy. He says, very tellingly, in his letter of intent for the position:

> I have always been interested in
> educational questions and inquiries;
> to be allowed to lecture on these

44

would be a particular joy to me.
(SLFN, 77)

It is hardly odd that Nietzsche would use his chair in philosophy to tackle questions of education, for his very notion of philosophy means teaching to live. Nietzsche tried to free himself from mere philology by moving to philosophy. But Nietzsche came more and more to think that a real teacher or a real philosopher could not exist within the confines of a university. It was the strength of his convictions conspiring with the fortunes of ill health which finally led him from the unflowering groves of academe.

Though Nietzsche's earliest reflections on education did not have as background his full break with the traditions of Western philosophy, certainly his earliest criticisms are of a piece with the last. He criticized the theory and practice of scholarship, the condition of intellectual heteronomy engendered by science and state, the partialism of current practices. He objected to foundational principles of state and society which informed the schools: he objected to the increasing democratization of the schools, the failure to impart life as the genuine test of education, and the failure to lay the foundations for new creativity, new ways of life. Opposed to these practices, Nietzsche advocated an an ethical/educational ideal of creativity pertinent to the true aristocrats, whom he charged with being the meaning of the earth. The ultimate metaphysical, moral, and epistemological positions that Nietzsche suggested make sense of these criticisms. There is no truth, there is only man seeking meaningful man through lived interpretation. And finally, whatever the causes, whether a matter of integrity or medicine, Nietzsche acted in accordance with the positions he held about educational institutions: he took philosophy outside the purview of the world he objected to, and set his books aloft like birds, knowing that "It is the stillest words that bring on the storm. Thoughts that come on doves' feet guide the world." (EH, 219)

In writing about Nietzsche, it is tempting to present one's arguments strictly in terms of his well-turned phrases. It is important, of course, to resist this connect-the-quotes style. Yet at this point I would like to let Nietzsche speak for himself yet one more time in spite of the fact that the last paragraph has all the earmarks of a final summation. In The Gay Science, Nietzsche writes: "I often look back in wrath at the most beautiful things that could not hold me — because they could not hold me." (GS, 247) Though not just then speaking of the universities, it is not hard to imagine Nietzsche feeling deep

45

ambiguity about the universities.   Schools were in a sense his home, and they opened horizons which his family life could never have offered. Yet Nietzsche found them wanting.   The university limited its own horizon, wasting man, wasting futures. Nietzsche's expressed anger represents the lament of a homeless wanderer: why couldn't you have held me!   We are all richer because nothing did seem to hold Nietzsche. This is an integral part of his lesson.   For even if the universities had not been guilty of all Nietzsche's charges, one would still have to move beyond them. There is little repose in Nietzsche. The following discussion shows the metaphysical importance of his eternal _agon_.

Chapter 3

THE CONTEST AND EDUCATION

> In short, dear friend, one
> can't go one's way independently
> enough. Truth seldom resides
> where temples are built and
> priests ordained for her.
>
> Nietzsche
> (NSP, 6)

The pervasive adversarial relations that Nietzsche maintained arose, it seems to me, not merely as affairs of a poseur, but as matters of human autonomy and meaning. I would like to suggest that at the heart of all Nietzsche's thinking about education is the contest, contest with oneself, with others, and with the world. The contest as an opportunity for self-reflection and self-appropriation provides man with the means of establishing identity. It was seen in the previous chapter that Nietzsche thought man's ideal rested immeasurably high above him. No ideal is achieved through mere living, but only through the active contest, through striving like gods, to put it in Nietzsche's dramatic language. Moreover, Nietzsche insists on the value of the contest, not specifically for the discernment of truth, but for the aggrandizement of life in all its capacities, and thus in all aspects of human meaning and identity.

Having seen the criticisms Nietzsche made of philosophy and university education generally, we are now in a position to examine the positive side of his philosophy of education. Contrary to the ideal of philosophy as theoretical metaphysics, Nietzsche charges philosophy with giving example of how to live, that is, how to establishing meaning in life. Contrary to the mechanical perpetuation of preordained ideology by the universities, Nietzsche suggested the creative ethic of amor fati. The cornerstone of this ethic is the contest, active engagement with opposition. Of course, knowledge remains a basic component of the quest for the noble way of life, yet this truth is not of the abstract, disinterested kind. This truth must be truth which is felt in the blood. The contest is not only an intellectual contest, but a contest of the quality of all life, of all meaning. The irreducible advantage of the contest is experience. And to the extent that the contest provides that experience, Nietzsche looks to it as the guiding notion of philosophy, of education, of life itself.

47

Baudelaire, Sartre says, admitted that there were three sorts of respectable beings: "the priest, the warrior and the poet. Knowing, killing and creation." (1) And though the parallel is not entirely exact, Nietzsche conflates these three in his overman and would have that one wage all their contests. Certainly Nietzsche waged all three kinds of battles in his own life. There was the struggle against traditional metaphysics. There was his struggle with Socrates. There was, too, the struggle of Dionysus against the Crucified. In what follows, it will be seen how Nietzsche envisions the nature of the contest, some of the contests he admired, and how his books beautifully exemplify the spirit of the contest between master and student, between author and reader. Moreover, it will be seen that the metaphysical vision that Nietzsche suggested is completely conducive to the contest. These topics range throughout his books, and no one book captures the whole of the emphasis on the contest, neither does any one book lack some kind of contest. Zarathustra may profitably be singled out, though remarks from his other books will be examined. One of the signal elements of Nietzsche's philosophy of education is the expected repudiation of the teacher. Zarathustra provides a good example of how Nietzsche actively sought the surpassing of the teacher. His own metaphysical vision, again, reinforces this contest inasmuch as he advocates constant creativity. It will be noted briefly, too, that while there is a publicly stated insistence on the repudiation of the teacher at all costs, Nietzsche's own biography shows the tension of a man caught between seeking and repudiating followers.

In Irrational Man, William Barrett points out that the Greek word for virtue, arete, clearly reflects Ares, the god of battle. He remarks further that "Classical civilizations rested on the recognition of power, and the relations of power, as a natural and basic part of life." (2) Nietzsche, too, recognized the interplay of power in Greek civilization and mourned its passing from modern society. Through his writings, he advocated a return to a culturally pervasive agon. Even his positive remarks on asceticism, seen in the previous chapter, are to be understood in terms of their praising the contest. There are thousands of remarks that could be adduced in testimony of Nietzsche's militaristically stylized orientation towards the contest, for he put the contest at the heart of friendship, of knowing oneself, of writing (Nietzsche's fascination with style can be understood as a fascination with the contest of language: "All who do not understand some kind of trade in weapons — tongue and pen included as weapons — become servile." (HATH, I, 124)), of beauty, of the desire for distinction, etc. In short, Nietzsche

48

put the contest at the heart of human experience. If what there is, metaphysically speaking, is power, then the contest is the manifestation and test of power.

Much has been made of Nietzsche's possible connections with the National socialist movement. This is not at all surprising since Nietzsche uses militaristic and ambiguous language. (3) For all the ambiguity in what that language means for concrete lived experience, there is still, clearly, an exaltation of war and warlike activities (and this for the benefit they render in making man aware of his existence and in urging him on to a fuller and more vital existence). Indeed, it would even seem that Nietzsche thought that man knew himself as an individual only through the contest:

> What one knows of oneself. —
> As soon as one animal sees another
> it measures itself against it in its
> mind, and men in barbarous ages did
> likewise. From this it follows that
> every man comes to know himself almost
> solely in regard to his powers of defence.
> (D, 134; cf. GM, 70, where Nietzsche
> says that the measurement of man against
> man might form thinking as such.)

The possibility of knowing oneself as an individual would seem to follow from being able to set oneself apart from another, looking for differences. And the adversative is the method of establishing these differences, whether the specific contest be physical, mental, or a combination of both.

If one knows oneself and can achieve distinction only through the adversative, it is an understatement that the contest is crucial to the possibility of human legitimacy and authenticity. Thus can one make sense of Nietzsche's trenchant aphorism appearing in one of his last works, but whose tone is evident in the entire corpus: "From the military school of life. — What does not kill me makes me stronger." (TI, 23) Victory spells the conquest of some feature of experience, and Nietzsche would have man become victorious in all realms of experience.

To be faithful to human experience and meaning, the contest must be structured into the very process of education. The educational process, therefore, must be literally agonal. That said, it would be well to point out that Nietzsche did not necessarily locate the value of the contest in the result of the contest, such that if one lost, one gained nothing. He located the value of the contest in the very struggle on behalf of a cause. Accordingly, he says: "The value of a thing sometimes lies not in what one attains with it, but in what one pays for it." (TI, 92) For example, one may not achieve any clear material gains in grappling with the existential question, but clearly there is merit in its pursuit since upon this question depends the determination of the meaning of human existence.

Nietzsche finds the hallmarks of moral complacency too prevalent in his society, in its unreflective acceptance of traditional moral values, in its ideology of eternally existing and immutable truth, in its socially democratic doctrine, in its educational policies which generate not whole human beings but parts for the machinery of a ruling ideology. Counterposed to this complacency, he offers the image of the creative man engaged in a continual struggle with himself (with the eddy of desires that Nietzsche conceives him to be), with his fellow man (with respect to the desire to be free of their dictatorial valuation), and with the world (in acceptance, for example, of the doctrine of the eternal return). Such a vision hangs on the cornerstone of the contest, of man locked into an eternal battle with the conditions of his existence. To remain faithful to the earth, to remain faithful to the human condition, one has to accept the conditions of the contest, else one risks decadence.

In Twilight's preface, Nietzsche says: "What could be more necessary than cheerfulness?" (TI, 21) He then purports to achieve this cheerfulness via war, by sounding out the "eternal idols" which have dominated the development of civilization. This consideration is of a piece with his essay on Schopenhauer, composed fourteen years earlier, in which he says: "Basically, you see, cheerfulness is only to be found where there is victory, and this applies to the works of all true thinkers as it does to every work of art." (SE, 16) The contest results in the victorious state of human cheerfulness, the condition of overfulness, the paradigmatic Nietzschean mood. This cheerfulness is the self-justifying condition, which on the grounds of lived experiences, means human well-being and self-fulfillment. But if such victory is the outcome of the successful contest, Nietzsche does caution that throwing oneself in the contest can sometimes be a sign of cowardice if motivated out of fear of social humiliation for failing to participate.

The contest functions as the form of the creative process. Even Zarathustra himself had to struggle long and hard with truths about the world before he could turn them to his advantage. So, too, would Nietzsche have the noble human being grapple with the world in all its aspects, such that he can abe master and dictator of them all. For if creativity follows from the condition of power, then creation itself is a contest, perhaps the most telling and taxing of all, since the paradigmatic meaning of creation is to bring something out of nothing. And since Nietzsche would arrogate to man all the predicates of god, then it would seem that he is putting man in complete charge of the world. If man cannot

bring something _ex nihilo_, then at least he can bring _meaning_ from
the possibility of man. (4)

In the course of the contest one must make sure that one
has the proper opponents. This insures that one will be tested to
the limit, that one will be forced to live life at the limits. To
engage in a contest with those less than one's peers benefits
neither side. One must flee flies, not fight them. (TSZ, 166)
The point here is that Nietzsche does not want the superior type
to expend himself on unworthy and debilitating opposition. The
higher type has already learned the lessons such opposition can
teach. There is no point in endlessly replaying the same lessons.

Not only has Western morality lost the notion of a proper
contest because of egalitarian moral positions, but Nietzsche
thinks that European society has lost a pivotal concept that he
found evidenced in Greek civilization:

> The Greeks have a word for indignation
> at another's unhappiness: this affect
> was inadmissible among Christian
> peoples and failed to develop, so that
> they also lack a name for this _more_
> _manly_ brother of pity. (D, 48)

Such a concept clearly revolves around an indignation at another's
allowing himself to be in a condition of failure, a failure to
endure and be victorious in a contest, whether it be of the
military or existential kind. It is evident here, too, as in so
many other places, that Nietzsche holds Christianity particularly
responsible for denaturing the contest.

Nietzsche's advice on the subject of one's relation to the
conquered and can be understood as being in opposition to pity.
Pity marks the end to a contest, whereas exultation in the
conquest, coupled with the kind of concept indicated above, serves
as a spur to further conquest. Nietzsche therefore urges that we
close our ears to the complaints of others. We can give neither
help nor comfort, nor keep listening to them:

> —unless, that is, we had acquired
> the art of the Olympians and henceforth
> _edified_ ourselves by the misfortunes
> of mankind instead of being made
> unhappy by them. (D, 91)

Of considerable interest in understanding Nietzsche's
notion of contest is his posthumously published fragment, _Homer's_
Contest. There, Nietzsche speaks about how firmly the contest was
entrenched at all levels of Greek civilization, how important it

was for the conduct of human affairs. He goes so far as to link the contest with the preservation of the state itself, therefore with the preservation of human life. (PN, 36) Of particular interest are his remarks to the effect that the very best victors in athletic contests were eventually barred from the competition, if not the city itself. In other words, the best of the competitors, holding their positions unbeatable and unchallenged, were eliminated altogether. Why?

> Why should no one be the best? Because
> then the contest would come to an
> end and the eternal source of life
> for the Hellenic state would be
> endangered. (PN, 36)

To be too long a victor stunts the possibility of new growth, of new victors. In short, Nietzsche thinks that a preponderance of victors means that the competition has come to stagnation, and since he locates the value of the contest in the process of the contest itself, then such stagnation spells decadence for humanity, even in the civilization of classical Greece. (Nietzsche even says that Christian vengeance against Rome was generated by the fatiguing sight of a continual conqueror.) (D, 42-43) The domination of a particular contest by one individual or by several individuals threatens the very conception of the contest. Nietzsche concludes:

> That is the core of the Hellenic notion
> of the contest: it abominates the
> rule of one and fears its danger; it
> desires, as a protection against the
> genius, another genius. (PN, 37)

As valuable as the genius is, the person whose vision engenders the 'truths' which dominate any civilization is not to go unchallenged. Insofar as the contest might be closed, finished or dominated exclusively, then the contest sees to be no contest at all and is as serious a threat to the ascendency of man as any given moral or intellectual idol.

One contest which gave birth to some of the dominant trends in Western philosophy was the contest which Nietzsche actively engaged from beginning to end, the agon of Socrates: dialectic. From his initial foray into intellectual history with Birth of Tragedy to Twilight (although also earlier and later than these books), Nietzsche exhibited fascination with the Socrates who could bring dialectic to the fore of Hellenic civilization, the cold, bright light of rationality opposing some deeper, more mysterious elements that particular civilization thrived in. In Birth of Tragedy, Nietzsche speculates about the changing form of Greek drama and attributes the rise of the rational, of the spoken

52

word over the musical, to Euripides as mask of Socrates. By the time he composed Twilight, Nietzsche was ready to explain the rise of Socrates. Socrates offered a new agon, a new contest. The dialectic he practiced seemed to be a panacea. (TI, 32-33) Indeed, it would not be many years before his student, Plato, offered a solution to human woe in the form of dialectician kings. Even if the old forms of contest could not endure in the face of crumbling political conditions, still individuals could seek mastery, and claim victory through the rarefied practice of reason. One might say, with Nietzsche, that this idea took hold with a vengeance in the West, shaping forms of thinking and living. It will not be necessary to follow out how Nietzsche thought dialectic transformed Greek culture. Rather it should be noted that he thought the rise of dialectic was consistent with Greek practice insofar as the Greeks adopted it as a form of agon. To be sure, this form of agon continues today unabated, with all sides advocating certain claims of truth in the face of repudiation and denial of those claims. And yet it is not the only form of contest; it cannot teach us all the lessons life has to offer. Nietzsche's criticism revolves around this point. Socrates lived the kind of partialized life we saw Nietzsche reject in university education. Restoration of complete life, of meaning in all realms of life, involves lessons other than those that dialectic has to offer.

Nietzsche's own contests, to be sure, are with the dominant moral valuations spawned with the origin of rational dialectic and decadent religion. These, he imagines, attempted an estimation of the value of life. At the very least, they attempted to structure the meaning of life. Since Nietzsche held that the value of life could not be estimated, given its infinite vista of meaning, he attempted to move beyond good and evil, beyond the constricting reign of prevalent morality, indeed, of moral systems altogether. All Nietzsche's writing seems to flow from his moral concerns, his concern with the value of life. Consequently, though he wrote about epistemology, metaphysics, and even logic, it is clear that Nietzsche's primary concern was of an axiological nature. Thus, when he posits that there is no truth (WP, 259, 331, 470, 480, 522, 540, 616, 974), he does so not only because he objected to the schema of Western metaphysics, but also, even primarily, because he sought thereby to liberate man. With respect to the first point, Nietzsche understood that in order to make any meaningful statement about being as a whole, the description offered by a philosopher had to be performatively consistent, i.e., must also apply to itself. And Nietzsche thought that this had not been done, could not be done because human knowing and language could not get beyond the level of interpretation. With respect to the latter point, Nietzsche sought to abandon Western metaphysics, the attempts to conquer truth, so to speak, because such a vision limited the possible interpretations man might creatively live if there were in fact

53

one truth. While these two kings of objections are not contradictory and, in fact, perhaps complement one another, one cannot help but think that it is his moral concerns that prompted Nietzsche to his reconsideration of Western, Socratic thought. The order of his writings might tend to bear this out, too, since many of his epistemologically oriented writings come later.

The task that Nietzsche set himself was a demanding one. He describes his task thus in a reflection in Ecce Homo on his essays about Schopenhauer and Wagner:

> What I was fundamentally trying to
> do in those essays was something
> altogether different from psychology;
> an unequaled problem of education,
> a new concept of self-discipline,
> self-defense to the point of hardness,
> a way to greatness and world historical
> tasks was seeking its
> first expression. (EH, 280)

Knowing the importance of the contest, knowing the liabilities of the contest, in retrospect Nietzsche formulated his task in terms of a contest with the given ideologies of life. No less than their review, dismantling, and surpassing would suffice to restore man to the capability of new contests, new educative experiments. The unequaled problem of education is the problem of educating man in a worthy morality through the notion of the contest, or as Nietzsche' puts it elsewhere, 'self-overcoming.' This problem of education is essentially a problem of philosophy insofar as the philosopher is conceived by Nietzsche as the paradigmatic 'attempter' or 'experimenter' (BGE, 52) who will give example in lived experience of the possibility of human creativity.

Though able to identify this as the educational problem, Nietzsche recognizes that "It will take unspeakable toil to replace the guiding thought of our present educational system which has its roots in the Middle Ages and sees as its educational ideal the medieval scholar." (SE, 80) The toil is unspeakable because of its magnitude. The Nietzschean ethic of self-overcoming maintains continual, adversative effort at its center. When Darwin looked long at nature he saw endless struggle at the level of species. When Nietzsche looked long at mankind he saw nothing but cessation of struggle. Man no longer lived, loved, or thought nobly. To the extent that mankind no longer willed struggle, to that extent his life is meaningless because the font of human meaning is the adversative situation.

The question of teaching is crucial to the philosopher for Nietzsche, as has been indicated elsewhere. Yet it is crucial for reasons not cited there as well. The question of teaching is crucial to the philosopher for Nietzsche, as has been indicated elsewhere. Yet it is crucial for reasons not cited there as well. The question of teaching is critical since philosophers have to avoid the pitfalls that their teaching may bring. Thus is to be understood Nietzsche's remark in a letter of his:

> Who knows how many generations must
> pass before people will come who can
> feel the whole depth of what I have
> done! And even then I am frightened
> by the thought of what unqualified
> and unsuitable people may invoke my
> authority one day. Yet that is the
> torment of every great teacher of
> mankind: he knows that, given the
> circumstances and the accidents, he
> can become a disaster as well as
> a blessing to mankind. (SLFN, 227)

As Nietzsche points out: "Without blind disciples the influence of a man and his work has never yet become great." (HATH, I, 127) Yet, paradoxically the condition to be feared is that "The followers of a great man often put their eyes out, so that they may be the better able to sing his praise." (HATH, II, 174) Greatness requires a certain amount of blindness in one's followers, and yet that blindness may spell the downfall of the great teacher, the great philosopher. Nietzsche's concern with the place of students in his philosophizing is more than just an attempt on his part to insure the success of his own immortality project. Presuming that one does not want to become a blight upon humanity, then it becomes crucial for a philosopher, whose domain is not only intellectual theory and speculation but also lived experience, to dwell on his educational methods such that his position will not be misinterpreted and form the basis for a denial of his position.

In short, Nietzsche's solution is the contest. At the heart of existence, Nietzsche envisions the contest, the rage to exist, the will to power. His conception of philosophy entails generation of a mode of living that exalts human be-ing. It is no surprise than Nietzsche exalts the contest. He does not seek to shoulder the burden of man, for it is uniquely man's prerogative to shoulder his own burden. The value of man resides in self-determination. Thus Nietzsche advocates 'become what you are,' and specifies nothing further. To those who would 'follow him,' he says very strongly:

> Type of my disciples.——To those human
> beings who are of any concern to me I
> wish suffering, desolation, sickness,
> ill-treatment, indignities——I wish that

> they should not remain unfamiliar with
> profound self-contempt, the torture
> of self-mistrust, the wretchedness of
> the vanquished: I have no pity for
> them, because I wish them the only thing
> that can prove today whether one is
> worth anything or not—that one endures.
> (WP, 910)

Nietzsche wishes such misery upon his students as a measure of their durability; the test becomes transforming suffering to one's advantage and incorporating both suffering and strength into the meaning of life. Thus is to be understood the insistence on inflicting hardship on 'followers.' He says further:

> I assess a man by the quantum of power and
> abundance of his will; not by its
> enfeeblement and extinction; I regard
> philosophy which teaches denial of the
> will as a teaching of defamation and
> slander—I assess the power of
> a will by how much resistance,
> pain, torture it endures and
> knows how to turn to its
> advantage; I do not account the
> evil and painful character of
> existence a reproach to it, but
> hope rather that it will one
> day be more evil and painful
> than hitherto. (WP, 206; cf. GM, 78)

In effect, Nietzsche is challenging man to his own self-education, because that follows from self-determination. In order to effect such an education, one must know the depths and the anguish of the contest, for it is endurance that is a spur to human creativity, to the highest human mastery. Nietzsche's praise of asceticism should be recalled here. Those who endure the rigors of the contest are those who merit being called masters. But here, as before, endurance is not the telos per se of the contest, but is the propadeutic to creation.

With this survey of the central place of the contest in Nietzsche's' thought and its implications for the philosophical endeavor in place, one would do well to turn to Zarathustra, the book which Nietzsche considered his most enduring and which shows the function of the contest in matters of education.

Laurence Lampert traces Zarathustra's actions as teacher and his final relations with his disciples. (7) Lampert quite rightly argues that in the course of the dramatic action, Zarathustra becomes increasingly guarded and subtle about himself and his teaching despite all the apparent excess of his behavior. He becomes, in the course of the book's progression, increasingly silent, finally abandoning disciples altogether since the lessons of the will to power and eternal return do not require them. (8) In any event, it would seem that the students could not know them, or to speak more accurately could not know them as lived experience. Lampert thinks that Zarathustra finally abandons all attempts at teaching, this being particularly evident in Book IV. After integrating the gift-giving virtue with the need to receive himself, Zarathustra only awaits worthy hearers, in solace, in vain in this book, though without desperation. As Lampert says: "The audience provided for his teaching gradually shrinks from all to none. (9) He concludes:

> While Zarathustra loses his disciples
> completely, he retains the gift giving
> virtue, though in devalued
> form. The disciples cannot receive
> the gift of his teaching and he no
> longer needs to give it. After the
> gift giving virtue has been eclipsed
> and Zarathustra, no longer all sun,
> receives life's teaching, the greatest
> virtue is not to give that teaching
> but to enjoy it. Joy needs no heirs.
> (TSZ, 10)

While it is certainly true that if Nietzsche's teaching is the wisdom of the will to power, then the import of Zarathustra is that the disciples will not understand and so they must be renounced, the parting being dictated by the incompatibility of Zarathustra's wisdom and their needs. It seems too much, however, to maintain that Zarathustra abandons teaching altogether. While it is true that Zarathustra finally does live his teaching and not attempt further proslytization, one wonders what the book as a whole could mean, what it could be if not an attempt at education. The character of the book does undergo a transformation from public teacher to private sage, (11) yet given Nietzsche's entire corpus the book cannot be understood but as an attempt at education, at teaching through showing by way of example of Zarathustra's life, by depiction, not by rational argumentation.

Lampert maintains that the most drastic change in Zarathustra during the course of his existential journal is the "recognition that the gift of knowing cannot be bestowed." (12) The testimony of Zarathustra's life in teaching clearly shows

57

this, but nevertheless the language of the whole book in its manner remains educational in intent since it shows by example the kind of lied experience which is necessary for an appropriation of truths about the human condition. These cannot be given by a scholar in a classroom, they cannot be given by Zarathustra himself in the marketplace. They can be learned only by oneself.

The fact that Zarathustra lived ten years in mountain solitude before arriving at the need to teach the overman is indicative of the kind of experience required to arrive at such a vision. In adopting the vision of the eternal return, Zarathustra had to return to the same solitude, Lampert quite rightly recognizes that:

> his passage from giver to enjoyer is
> itself a teaching, Zarathustra is
> a failure as a teacher. The reasons
> for this failure are important because
> the portrayal of the failed teacher
> is itself a teaching. In these
> dramatics the true teacher in Thus
> Spoke Zarathustra teaches. He
> takes as his audience the whole world
> but he speaks to that audience
> obliquely through one who never fully
> learned the middle way between direct
> speaking and silence. Zarathustra is
> no Socrates, and Nietzsche no reticent
> Plato. It is not through Zarathustra's
> successes as a teacher that Nietzsche
> teaches his deepest truths of the
> order of things, but through his
> failures. (13)

In Twilight of the Idols, Nietzsche says: "Our true experiences are not garrulous," i.e., speaking vulgarizes. (TI, 82) Even with his heart full of desire to enlighten mankind, Zarathustra comes to recognize that his wisdom cannot be transmitted through verbal articulation. His is a wisdom that can only come through the struggle on the experiential level. Thus, if Nietzsche has Zarathustra become reticent, still he speaks, but only as a way of challenge to begin this experiential struggle, to recognize the human condition for what it is. If the wisdom of man is not garrulous, still it can be pointed to, and in this respect Zarathustra remains a teacher par excellence.

The method of instruction is the depiction of his own self education, his own endurance, and finally his own conquest of those obstacles to self appropriation. For though he imagined himself wise, at the opening Zarathustra was a very unwise man. He descended from the mountain to teach. Why? What made him think that anyone could understand him? The people of the marketplace cannot understand him because they do not have, and do not even see as desirable, the same experiential basis for comprehension. Even the person whom Zarathustra first met on his descent, the saint, a higher human being, could not understand him. Zarathustra ultimately passed by him in silence, not telling him what would undermine his life, that god was dead. If the saint, conceived as a higher form of human being, does not understand him, what makes Zarathustra think that the commoners of the marketplace will? How can he teach them? In the end he cannot. He must toss his pronouncements to the wind (that is, to the future), and then he must retreat, for ultimately his position demands addressing only the few, and even then, paradoxically, his position demands the renunciation of the teacher.

Harold Alderman also recognizes the key role of teacher in Zarathustra. He claims, quite rightly I think, that the incident of Zarathustra's first disciple, the dead tight-rope walker, recapitulates the metamorphoses of the spirit, Zarathustra's first speech immediately following the Prologue. This personal metamorphosis enables Zarathustra to realize that he cannot be dependent upon his audience, that he must in fact flee from them. They do not want the struggle, they want the last man, the man who has invented happiness. Thus, Zarathustra recognizes that he must seek disciples no longer, but companions. Though he continues to address his 'disciples,' his ultimately intention is to speak through the disciples to his companions, though they may not even be living yet.

Alderman claims that tied to this theme is Nietzsche's exploration of the limit and range of human speech: "In that exploration, Nietzsche tries to tell us (and to show us) how what can be meaningfully said can be said. And finally he tries to show us that there is a limit beyond which all forms of human language begin to fail. Through the exploration of that limit, Nietzsche demonstrates "the crucial roles of dance, laughter, and song in the human communication of the unspeakable." (15) The point is similar to that made by Lampert, that language is not the medium of Zarathustra's wisdom, though it can show the way to wisdom. Indeed, the rest of the book shows how Zarathustra strives not to tell but to represent a mode of appropriation of the truths of being. Finally, Zarathustra seems to communicate not with other individuals but with the world itself, and this can be done better without the chatter and incomprehension of students.

Nietzsche has Zarathustra enter into a dialogue with the world itself, and this strains the limits of language such that Zarathustra does come to recognize the impoverishment of all oratory. Finally, Zarathustra addresses no one in the book but 'humanity,' and even then only its wisest men. (17) The wise

59

teacher must recognize the limits of his educational methods. Zarathustra recognizes that his philosophical truths are not compatible with a method of public oration, speaking to all that happen by. Rather, his 'doctrine' demands an intense experiential basis. Thus, he withdraws from actively seeking out disciples and instead wards off followers, presuming thereby to use masks and deceptions as instruments of selecting out those fit as higher human beings. This subject of duplicity is taken up in the next chapter.

For Zarathustra, finally, the animals are the real interlocuteurs if he has any at all. They are neither the disciples of Part II nor the superior men of Part IV. (18) There is no forcing him as a character back into the cave as Plato stipulated in the Republic for his philosopher-educators. Not even the 'higher' men can lure him into becoming their teacher. If anything, he agrees to be their jester. (19) One day, though, they may become genuine students, which in the last analysis means for Nietzsche, being students of themselves. (20) The situation of Zarathustra is well described by Alderman:

> If the higher men want to learn as
> Zarathustra teaches himself, then he
> makes room for them. But like every
> great philosopher, Zarathustra talks
> in the final analysis only to
> himself. Every other conversation is
> only preparation for that more
> personal monolog.

Indeed, the teaching of Nietzsche was characterized as being an exhortation to engage in existential struggle in order to test oneself. Primarily, then, education is personal, and one must see the contest as the chief mode of personal aggrandizement. The teacher is but instrument. Zarathustra did not want followers. He wanted individuals surpassing him in his wisdom. He wanted his own repudiation.

Nietzsche's corpus is rife with remarks advocating the repudiation of the teacher.(22) For only in the repudiation of the ideals and practices of the teacher can there be any possibility of self-created meaning. Repudiation puts one in a condition of existential solitude, certainly psychical if not physical, in which creativity and living become identical. Nietzsche takes the drive to emulation or identification with the teacher as a sign of weakness. In fact, he identifies strength with the ability to drive away (WP, 655), and thus is to be understood Part IV of Zarathustra with its emphasis on Zarathustra's test of pity at the sight of men effectively crippled by their limited appropriation of his teaching.

Of course, if this be the official pronouncement of Nietzsche, that the teacher must drive away, and demand the repudiation of anyone who would seek to 'follow' him,' then it is also the source of tremendous irony with respect to his own personal life. He recognized his isolation and suffered from loneliness. Even though his books demanding surpassing, he wanted, but found no readers. He wanted readers, and he did not want readers. He feared the misinterpretation of his work. He feared descending into the marketplace to speak. He knew that profound experience was not garrulous, yet he wrote over seventeen books and left behind a vast nachlass. His philosophy demanding the self-determination of individuals, yet he also knew that without disciples, no man has great influence. (Cf. HATH, I, 127, 373) What he said of Schopenhauer he feared for himself: first he suffered for a long time with no readers, and when his readers did come, they were of the wrong kind. (SE, 86) Nietzsche knew that he required pupils and heirs, and yet in Zarathustra he bypasses them altogether. He speaks past them, he speaks to his future companions. Even if at the end of the book, Zarathustra is content to remain in his self-imposed isolation, still his author, Nietzsche, remains desperate for some kind of following. Thus, while Kaufmann makes a caustic remark about Peter Gast proclaiming Nietzsche hold even though Nietzsche had worried that some day he might be proclaimed holy, (23) he might equally well have made the remark at Nietzsche's expense, for in a letter to Franz Overbeck, Nietzsche himself said:

> I require so much from myself that
> I am ungrateful vis-a-vis the best
> work that I have done till now; and if
> I do not go to such an extreme that
> whole millenia will make their
> loftiest vows in my name, then in my
> own eyes I shall have achieved
> nothing. Meanwhile, I do not have
> a single disciple. (SLFN, 225)

I could equally well cite a letter to Malwida von Meysenbug:

> What I want, my son Zarathustra won't
> tell you. But he'll challenge you to
> figure it out, and perhaps you can.
> This much is certain: I wish to force
> mankind to decisions which will
> determine its entire future—and may yet
> happen that one day whole millenia will
> make their most solemn vows in my name.
> (NSP, 81)

Or again, in a letter in which he remarks on the independence of a genuine philosopher, Nietzsche says to his mother:

> ...also I am well enough acquainted
> with human nature to know how the
> judgment on me will have been
> reversed in fifty years time, and
> with what splendor of reverence your
> son's name will then shine, on account
> of the same things as those for which
> I have till now been mishandled and
> abused. (SLFN, 271)

While I have singled out Kaufmann here, it should be noted that other authors have made use, for purposes of irony, of Nietzsche's published aversion to being pronounced holy. (24)

When recognition finally came, in the form of George Brandes' correspondence and lectures, he was immensely gratified. Upon hearing of Brandes' enterprise, Nietzsche wrote: "North winds, it seems, bring me good cheer. Just imagine, they are blowing my way from as far off as Denmark." (NSP,117) By the time he wrote Ecce Homo, Nietzsche would flaunt what he took to be his impressive and wide-ranging readership and influence. (EH, 262) Even if Nietzsche feared being called holy, he did so only when he was assured of some danger of it happening.

Though he became infatuated with the possibility of success and influence among the intelligentsia, Nietzsche's ultimate doctrine must be that one demand, indeed that the teacher himself demand repudiation of the teacher! This does not preclude the possiblity that the teacher will be eminently influential, but will result that he serve only as a spur to the possibility of creativity on the part of the student. The teacher must warn the student against himself. Perhaps thus is to be understood Nietzsche's fear of being pronounced holy, that he will become some philosophical dictator who destroys the possibility of an open future, turning philosophical activity into an intellectual and moral spiderweb. The nature of his instruction must be centered on the contest, for in failing to understand the role of the contest one fails to understand human life at all, or at least Nietzsche's vision that the world thrives only in struggle, only when it does not become complacent about its convictions. The end of contest means the end of meaning.

The contest must be cultivated at all levels of development, taking into consideration the necessity for the right opponents, the proper timing and the like. The ideal of the contest, too, must seek the integration of all aspects of an individual. The individual, or at least the superior individual, must not become guilty of he partialism that Nietzsche thought typified the products of German schools. There must be a development of the individual's abilities, through the contest, in order to render him capable of meaning-full creation. To be sure, one of the hallmarks of Nietzsche's entire work is his insistence on man as creative being. He exalts the possibility of human transformation of self and world. Since there are many possibilities, there are many modes of contest, but they all point at the same thing: the rejection of the notion of an 'ideal' or fixed telos for man:

> The very obscure and arbitrary idea
> that mankind has a single task to
> perform, that it is moving as a whole
> towards some goal, is still very
> young. Perhaps we shall be rid of
> it again before it becomes a 'fixed
> idea.' (WP, 339) (25)

The repudiation of some fixed ideal towards which all men must move is central to all of Nietzsche's thought. Such a repudiation requires a certain destruction of past idols and truths. But the destruction is simply not enough, for the creation of new modes of living is the ultimate test of power. And the contest is the form of achieving this creation.

It is undoubtedly true that Nietzsche overemphasized the extent to which human achievement and meaning are matters of adversative conditions. The structure of human meaning revolves around experience, to be sure, but educative experience need not always be a matter of torture and pain. Lessons of meaning can be learned by the heart as well as by will. For example, it will likely never be possible that man has complete dominion of the universe through mechanical means, but it is easy enough to hold the university in dominion by love. As an antidote to complacency in education, Nietzsche's remarks are well taken. Yet it is not entirely clear from what he has said that a adversative education is necessarily the precondition for conquest. After all, some victories can be Phyrric.

In the education of man, Nietzsche seeks the dominion of man, not dominion by Nietzsche. There are no easy formulae for human accomplishment in his books, no rationalization of the status quo, no social or metaphysical consolations. His insights have opened up the future to our creativity to be sure, but that future can have the aspect of a desert. (TSZ, 215; WP, 603) To be a student of Nietzsche, one must be a student of one's own life. There are, it seems no universal answers to the problems of human living and meaning. There are only men seeking meaningful life. As a matter of will, adversity, and conquest, the contest gives man the form of self-appropriation. It is this that is to be admired in Nietzsche, the unflinching will to meaningfulness. And if we learn from his contests, we learn this: our education, the possibility of meaningful life will issue from our contests. What we exert ourselves on behalf of ourselves signifies what we are and what we mean.

Chapter 4

THE TEACHER AND THE LIE

> And, after all, what is a lie? Tis but
> The truth in masquerade, and I defy
> Historians—heroes—lawyers—priests to put
> A fact without some leaven of a lie.
>
> Byron
> (1)

Over and above the sometimes puzzling aphoristic nature of Nietzsche's works, one finds instances of apparent deception. Or at least one finds Nietzsche calling attention to possible deceptions. (BGE, 50n) The issue of understanding these lies and masks is crucial to understanding Nietzsche. Masks and lies are used, in his line of thinking, by those able to accept such truths as the eternal return and to ward off those persons unable to comprehend such interpretive truths, thereby preventing a misappropriation of that 'truth.' The masking process for Nietzsche is a basic activity and prerogative of the superior type.

What follows in this chapter is an examination of the use of masks and lies as a form of the contest, symbolizing for Nietzsche, power, artistry, and even play. Lies and masks function as one form of repudiation which Nietzsche actively advocated as belonging to the form of the educational process. Lies and masks, in this sense, correct some of the educational failures pointed out in Chapter II. For example, lies and masks allow the possibility of solitude that Nietzsche saw as so desirable for creativity and which he saw little of in university education. Throughout the discussion, too, it will be seen that contrary to their apparent natures, masks and lies have both a concealing and a revealing aspect. It is this ambiguity that Nietzsche uses as the center of gravity for his use of masks and lies. Moreover, it will be seen that new philosophers, new interpreters and creators must necessarily seem to speak in lies since 'lies' exist only in relation to the 'truths' of an existing civilization. The coinage of new interpretations, in accordance with Nietzsche's exhortations would seem to require, then, the lie. Moreover, it will be seen that masking/lying is integral to any social role. It will be seen, finally, that Nietzsche thinks

65

that the objections hitherto advanced against lying/masking are couched in public utility rather than any genuine moral argument or sentiment against falsity per se.

The notion of lies and masks, then, are intimately connected with the notion of the contest at the level of creative, new interpretations and the form of social interaction between teacher and student. The lie and the mask are spurs to creativity, providing as they do the opportunity of a certain kind of agonal lesson, a lesson available only to those who understand the revealing and concealing aspect of the lie/mask.

Walter Kaufmann published, just before he died, a book as the second volume of a series called Discovering the Mind. Therein he ranks Nietzsche as one of the principal discoverers of the mind, claiming as his chief contributions: consciousness as surface, the theory of the will to power, psychology of world views, pioneering psychohistory, and the philosophy of masks. In his remarks on masks, Kaufmann shows how they (as well as role-playing and dissimulation) are tied to profundity. My work, prepared before the appearance of that volume makes no conclusions contrary to Kaufmann's claims. Rather it expands the discussion to consider how the mask and the lie function in an educational sense. And they function, to repeat, as a contest. Kaufmann attempts to show that (a) Nietzsche did not think the use of masks inauthentic and evil, (2) (b) that masks and role playing can be reconciled with intellectual conscience as long as the parties involved recognize them for what they are, (3) and (c) that Nietzsche links masks and profundities properly because what is profound is often difficult and bears the semblance of a mask. (4) These three subjects will be considered in this chapter though no further specific reference will be made to Kaufmann's rather cursory presentation.

It seems to me that the discussion of the lie and the mask is best considered in the context of Nietzsche's agonal philosophy of education. Nietzsche, for the most part, centers his arguments on behalf of lying in the benefit they can have for the advancement of individual power. For Nietzsche, lies and masks are tests of power, tests of autonomy (not Kantian autonomy but autonomy in a the broad, etymological sense of 'self-legislating') such that he thinks the highest individuals are those who can be the most deceptive, the most hidden. Sissela Bok argues against lies on the assumption that lies are not neutral in themselves, that they interfere with autonomy, trust and integrity. According to Nietzsche, however, lies and masks make such traits possible!

66

Before going any further, the following senses of the lie must be distinguished: the lie which functions as a veil of illusion (horizons interpreted for the possibility of human conduct; such is the use in the Birth of Tragedy) and the lie as an intentionally deceptive piece of falsehood. The former might be called a metaphysical lie and is intimately associated by Nietzsche with art. The latter might be considered a moral lie. This distinction, however, might be merely theoretical since it may happen that the latter can come to function as the former. Nietzsche thought that life required horizons of meaning. And since there are no truths of the idealist variety for him, then it would seem that any interpretation which posited itself as an enduring truth for human life (and knew itself this way) would be a lie. Nonetheless, these interpretations give the desired metaphysical horizon to life, and give man a contest for life.

Nietzsche is concerned with both species of lies (and of masks that would function in the same way). Ultimately both can fuse in that they become part and parcel of the vision of the world that emerges from an individual's agonal activities. This fusion is further strengthened by the consideration that it is the noble individual as liar, as artist who comes to furnish the metaphysical lies of a civilization. The ultimate meaning of the lie is its meaning as a contest for purposes of life, and it is in such meaning that Nietzsche grounds its justification.

That Nietzsche thought that some structure of meaning, some veil of illusion was necessary for the possibility of human action and productivity can be seen in the following remark, which is typical on the subject: "In short, I still live; and life, in spite of ourselves, is not devised by morality' it demands illusions, it lives by illusion..." (HATH, I, 3) Art functions as a masking activity:

> Hence art must conceal or transfigure
> everything that is ugly—the painful,
> terrible, and disgusting elements
> which in spite of every effort will
> always break out afresh in accordance
> with the very origin of human nature.
> (HATH, II, 92)

It might even be said that metaphysics, morality, religion, and science are all forms of illusions or lies in that they impose non-necessary interpretations on the world. Indeed, Nietzsche writes that to solve the task imposed by life:

> man must be a liar by nature, he must
> be above all an artist. And he is one:
> metaphysics, religion, morality, science—

67

all of them only products of his will to
art, to lie, to flight from 'truth,'
to negation of 'truth.' (WP, 853)

Accordingly, the great, creative individual is the one who is the
artist, who invents new forms of science, morality, and even
religion. These are all species of lies inasmuch as they are,
again, non-necessary interpretations posing as Truth.

Nietzsche explicitly states that with respect to the
highest types, "Whatever is profound loves masks; what is most
profound even hates image and parable." (BGE, 50-51) If one
considers the import of such a dictum for education, one realizes
that not only do creative individuals generate veils of illusion
for the possibility of life, but they likewise mask themselves.
It would seem that in philosophy's task of education, there must
be an emphasis on creativity (to generate these new veils as
meaning for oneself if not for others) and on instructing in how
to mask oneself. The student, then, would have before him the
task of interpreting and seeing behind particular masks, lies, and
postures in order to make some kind of determination of what these
things mean and conceal, for it is known beforehand that the
teacher hides his profundity. Unlike Zarathustra of the Prologue,
the teacher does not rush to the marketplace bellowing his
knowledge to every passerby. On the contrary, access to the
teacher comes only through struggling at the same experiential
level as the teacher in order to understand why he has come to use
the particular lies and masks that he has.

As mentioned earlier, Bok holds that lies are not in
themselves ethically neutral and are ultimately destructive in
themselves. They undermine authority, respect, and trust, however
nobly they are used. Nietzsche, interestingly enough, does not
seem to hold that lies are neutral either. They have a decided
impact on the people using them. But for him, they are measures
of power! In one place, he cynically, but for all that perhaps
truthfully, remarks that people generally tell the truth because
they are not intelligent enough to lie:

Why do most people speak the truth in
daily life?--Assuredly not because a
god has forbidden falsehood. But
firstly, because it is more convenient,
as falsehood requires invention,
conceit and memory. (HATH, I, 72;
cf. D, 176)

That is to say that they are not intelligent enough to coordinate
all their lies and remain undetected by others. Conceived as
instruments of education, as measuring the power of both teacher
and student, lies and masks cannot be neutral: they are the

68

indicators and measurement of power. Thus one understands Nietzsche's remark:

> When a philosopher keeps silent, it can
> be a loftiness of the soul; when he
> contradicts himself, it can be love;
> a politeness which tells lies is possible
> in men of knowledge. (TI, 100)

In fact, Nietzsche even thinks that lies and masks might be a kind of play for the noble type:

> In a conversation you can watch one of
> the participants busy setting a trap
> into which the other then falls—but he
> does it, not out of malice, as might be
> thought, but out of pleasure at his own
> artfulness. (D, 165)

Beyond these reasons, Nietzsche further considers why the lie is not as undesirable as some have claimed. In his notebooks, he remarked that it is not the lie per se which is objected to, but the evil consequences which follow from the lie. (WP, 342, PN, 45) That is, one objects not to the lie qua lie but to the possible ill results from having been taken in by the lie. This notion is developed in an interesting piece called "On Truth and Lies in a Normal Sense." Published only posthumously, but written in 1872, Nietzsche gives there the following definition of truth:

> A movable host of metaphors, metonyms,
> and anthropomorphisms: in short, a sum
> of human relations which have been
> poetically and rhetorically intensified,
> transferred, and embellished, and which,
> after long usage, seem to a people to
> be fixed, canonical, and binding.
> Truths are illusions which we have
> forgotten are illusions; they are metaphors
> that have become worn out and have been
> drained of their sensuous force, coins
> which have lost their embossing and are
> now considered as metal and no longer
> as coins. (PT, 84)

Nietzsche's conception of truth is quite of a piece with his metaphysics of interpretation. 'Truth' is understood as the sum of metaphors (interpretations) which have hardened into apparently determinate fixations, eternal representations as it were. In the beginning, all truths were the result of metaphoric interpretations; metaphoric because there is no standard of eternal and immutable truth against which to measure them, and interpretations because all knowledge, all truth is the function of the human imposition of power on particular world experience. Accordingly, 'lies' would at one level seem to be only deviation in metaphoric interpretation, being a refusal to participate in the received wisdom as it is given.

It would seem, according to this same unfinished work, that Nietzsche thought that agreement on basic interpretations provided some kind of theoretical groundwork for the possibility of human life in common. Imagining that men initially exist in a state of 'Hobbesian' relations, Nietzsche thinks that some kind of peace treaty resulted to mitigate at least the most flagrant aspects of bellum omni contra omnes. (PT, 84; cf HATH, I, 90) Puzzling that the drive for pure, disinterested truth could have arisen at all among men who sought to gain advantage over each other, Nietzsche further imagines that the first step of this peace treaty was establishing something that shall count as truth:

> That is to say, a uniformly valid and
> binding designation is invented for
> things, and this legislation of
> language likewise establishes the first
> laws of truth.

Following such a compact,

> the contrast between truth and lie
> appears here for the first time. The
> liar is a person who uses the valid
> designations, the words, in order to
> make something which is unreal appear
> to be real. He says, 'for example,'
> 'I am rich,' when the proper
> designation for his condition would
> be 'poor.' He misuses fixed
> conventions by means of arbitrary
> substitutions or even reversals of
> names.

The misuse, of course, of ordinary designations threatens the foundation of the social compact:

> If he does this in a selfish and
> moreover harmful manner, society
> will cease to trust him and will
> thereby exclude him. What men avoid
> by excluding the liar is not so much
> being defrauded as it is being harmed
> by means of fraud. Thus, even at
> this stage, what they hate is basically
> not the deception itself, but rather

70

            the unpleasant, hated consequences
            of certain sorts of deception.

The lie per se is not objected to. Delight and enjoyment in all
kinds of fiction and fantasy is evidence enough of this. What is
objected to is the possibility of suffering because of the lie.
Nietzsche posits the real incentive toward truth then:

> It is in a similarly restricted
> sense that man now wants nothing
> but truth: he desires the pleasant,
> life-preserving consequences of
> truth. He is indifferent towards
> those truths which are possibly
> harmful and destructive he is even
> hostilely inclined. (PT, 84)

Consequently, truth would seem to be a function of the desire to
live unharmed in society. At least, one would make one's
determinations of truth and falsity on that basis.

        It is clear that Nietzsche does not object to the lie per
se, for the lie is merely a recasting of the initial metaphors of
interpretation, and he demands new interpretations constantly, as
the result of his ethic of creativity. What others find
objectionable about the lie is that it harms them; that is to say,
it harms their ordered structure of meaning. At minimum it
challenges their world-view metaphor. At most it might disrupt
the possibility of human community at all. Nietzsche
concludes that the society of man must demand that all members
take the established 'truths' as immutable standards. In other
words, he says, society demands the duty of lying:

> according to a fixed convention,
> to lie with the herd and in a manner
> binding upon everyone. Now man of
> course forgets that this is the way
> things stand for him. Thus he lies
> in the manner indicated, unconsciously
> and in accordance with habits which
> are centuries old; and precisely by
> means of this unconsciousness
> and forgetfulness he arrives at his
> sense of truth. (PT, 84)

What then is 'truth?' Truth is a 'lie' that has been forgotten as
such. Society for its own purposes socializes its members to adopt
the interpretation beneficial to itself.

        In another note from the same year in which he composed
the above, Nietzsche expands his reflections about the lie:

> Man demands truth and fulfills this
> demand in moral intercourse with
> other men; this is the basis of all
> social life. One anticipates the
> unpleasant reciprocal lying. From
> this there arises the duty of
> truth. We permit epic poets to lie
> because we expect no detrimental
> consequences in this case. Assuming
> that it does no harm, the lie is
> beautiful and charming. Thus the priest
> invents myths for his gods which
> justify their sublimity. It is extra-
> ordinarily difficult to revive the
> mythical feeling of the free lie.
> Yet the great Greek philosophers dwell
> entirely within this justification of
> the lie. (PT, 27)

The lie, for Nietzsche, is not so much a strict contradiction of truth as it is a new interpretation, a break with the usage and designations of the existing community. In a sense, then, when he arrogates to the noble individual, to the teacher the right to lie (WP, 980) he effectively entrusts the teacher with the responsibility of new interpretations, the coinage of new truth. The ability to lie is assuredly not neutral in itself. For its first and foremost characteristic would indicate power sufficient to break with the existing convention called 'truth.' And secondly, if the lie is successful, it indicates power enough to separate from the herd without at the same time being detected in the break (which would incite the herd against one).

Nietzsche points out in a number of places that lies are instrumental in that when lived consistently, they become truths, become instead of masks, genuine visages. Ultimately, of course, this might be mere continuous self-deception. Nevertheless, Nietzsche says "There must be self-deception in order that this and that may produce great effects." (HATH, I, 71) The founders of religions, he says, never awaken from their condition of self-deception. After a long and obstinate desire to appear as something, providing that one's initial capabilities are equal to the task, it would appear that one does in fact become that something: the mask finally molds. (HATH, I, 70) Put in an educational context, the lie or the mask can be an instrument by which one advances, sets oneself apart from the mask, and finally, protects oneself from the crowd. (5)

That Nietzsche did not object to the lie per se is also evident in one of his last books, The AntiChrist. In that polemic, Nietzsche remarks that the priest, almost by definition,

72

tells lies (primarily the lie that truth exists). By way of comment, Nietzsche says: "—Ultimately the point is to what end a lie is told. That 'holy' ends are lacking in Christianity is my objection to its means." (AC, 175) Christianity uses, like all great religions and philosophies, lies in the course of its advancement. But Nietzsche explicitly says here that he objects not to the lie itself, but to the ends to which the lies are used. He says: "It does indeed make a difference for what purpose one lies: whether one preserves with a lie or destroys with it." (AC, 179) This book, composed in 1888, is in agreement with the unpublished notes of 1872: the lie is objectionable not in se but in its usage.

In Twilight of the Idols, Nietzsche remarks ironically that no teachers have ever doubted their right to tell lies, thus establishing an apparent contradiction between their professed ideal of making man more moral and their decidedly immoral means. (TI, 59; cf., 141) This jibe, however, attempts to show a contradiction between ideals and practices of certain moralists. It does not undermine Nietzsche's theoretical embracing of the lie.

Nietzsche thinks that just as the actor and writer perform, thinking always of their audience, so too must the teacher proceed. This concern provides the entree into the discussion of the lie with specific reference to the educator. To be sure, Nietzsche makes inexorable demands on the teacher. In an exceptional note, he writes:

> Assuming one thinks of a philosopher
> as a great educator, powerful enough
> to draw up to his lonely height a
> long chain of generations, then
> one must also grant him the uncanny
> privileges of a great educator. An
> educator never says what he himself
> thinks, but always only in relation
> to the requirements of those he
> educates. He must not be detected in
> this dissimulation; it is part of his
> mastery that one believes in his
> honesty. He must be capable of employing
> every means of discipline: some he
> can drive towards the heights with the
> whips of scorn; others, who are sluggish,
> irresolute, cowardly, vain, perhaps
> only with exaggerated praise. Such
> an educator is beyond good and evil;
> but no one must know it. (WP, 980;
> HATH, II, 280-281)

73

Here Nietzsche explicitly makes the connection between philosophical and educational activity. He claims that the teacher must take himself seriously only in relation to the needs of those whom he teaches. (Cf. HATH, I, 184; BGE, 79) Teacher, here, should be taken in its broadest sense, not just the sense of university educator. The masking of the teacher is an instrument of control, and the point of the masking is preservation of self-integrity and utility for education of others.

On the one hand, masks serve a protective function for the teacher; they ward off those who could not but go astray. On the other hand they can _also_ serve as "instructive signs which a writer [or teacher] gives to the discerning reader [or student] so that he may discover what the thinker is really about." (6) Alderman rightly points out:

> Nietzsche's use of masking devices as
> an integral part of his writing thus
> places the problem of interpretation
> right at the center of any response
> to his work. These devices—and this
> is intentional in Nietzsche—destroy
> once and for all the naive and realistic
> pretension that a book is a kind of
> thing-in-itself which the interpreter
> simply stares at neutrally in order
> to read off its intrinsic properties
> or meanings. (7)

In Chapter 3, it was pointed out that Nietzsche sought the repudiation or surpassing of the teacher by the student. Zarathustra gives ample evidence of this. In a wider sense, all his books, with their masks and lies, serve as instruments of the educational/philosophical contest. Nietzsche would ideally not have followers. He would, however, have contestants and opponents. Thus, the technique of his writing style embodies the techniques of masking to force the reader to engage him in order to understand, first of all, Nietzsche and, secondly, the reader himself. By understanding the particular contests, by understanding the particular masks and lies that a writer or opponent uses, one is in a position to understand what that writer or opponent is revealing. On the one hand, masks repel, but on the other hand they reveal the kind of contest that is being engaged in. And it would be the Übermensch who is ultimately the criterion against which roles, masks, and lies are measured. (8). Since it is the Übermensch who is by definition by person having the highest mastery of all possible roles, masks, and lies.

The privileges of the educator are grounded in the advance of power, symbolized in the overman. Insofar as the educator can advance the condition of mankind, he is permitted the instrument

74

of the lie and mask, for the very technique of the education of
mankind, the contest, does not presuppose that the student/pupil
will remain trapped by the lie. In fact, he will expect the
deception; he will expect to be deceived and will therefore be on
the lookout to avoid entrapment, thereby repudiating and
surpassing the teacher. Such a forewarning does not, eo ipso,
justify deceit. However, it does shift the course of the analysis
to see why deceit should be expected as a kind of regulative
principle.

Ultimately Nietzsche's justification of the lie is a kind
of paternalistic one, namely a lie undertaken on behalf of the
good of the deceived without his or her consent. Bok points out
that the traditional justification for this kind of lie is that
the deceived will agree to the necessity of the lie when fully
apprised of its necessity in such and such a situation. By way of
objection to this argument, she points out that consent does not
always follow. (9) If one examines the problem of the
paternalistic lie from the perspective of Nietzsche, one can see
that he would certainly agree that the paternalistic lie
presupposes too much if it depends upon the subsequent assent of
the deceived. However, in the case of Nietzschean instruction,
the student should expect deception and masking on the part of the
teacher. The lies are expedients. That a discovered lie
threatens the existing fabric of social relations is all to
Nietzsche's point. Thus does the learner spurn his teachers,
become aware of the solitude that is necessary for creation, and
begin the long journey to independence.

In terms of educational contest, everyone (or at least the
noble types) will use masks and lies in a mutually deceptive
manner. Bok raises this issue and wonders whether lying is
excusable in a mutually consensual, deceptive relationship since
apparently voluntary and terminable at will. (10) She concludes
that although the rules are known to all, the result of such
practice is coarsened judgment and diminished responsibility.
That the deceived is a liar adds nothing to the case against
deception, she maintains. By contrast, Nietzsche holds that the
relationship between individuals, particularly among the noble, is
always one of deception insofar as the deception is an instrument
of the agon (D, 119-120) It can only be reiterated that, having
acknowledged the necessity of lies and masks in advance, this form
of contest need not end in coarsened judgment and diminished
responsibility. On the contrary, it might well produce more
adeptness in the recognition and surpassing of masks and
deceptions.

It is probably unfair to compare Nietzsche with Bok on
other categories of lies since she is concerned with many kinds of
lies that he has no interest in, deception in medical therapy and
the like. However, it is interesting to see that once Nietzsche

shifts the criterion of judgment from reason and truth as classically understood to power, her arguments against certain kinds of lies would seem to fail. (This is not to maintain that the two concepts are entirely antithetical, for reason can quite clearly be an expedient of power.) Lies are justified on the grounds that they can be expedients of power. Not for all, to be sure, but for those whom Nietzsche identifies as true students and true philosophers. Consequently, in the education of man, the lie stands as one test of his ability to surpass the teacher and give indication of his likelihood for creation. As the contest of life progresses, Nietzsche sees that it is those who have broken free from the herd, those who have caught the lie can best shape the future, for hey have not mistaken interpretation for eternal and immutable truth.

On the heels of this discussion of the justifiability of the lie it may come as a surprise that one finds in Nietzsche the equally strong conviction that what is needed is not deception, but the most straightforward honesty as the highest mark of human integrity. For example, there is Nietzsche's praise of Lessing, which he gives by quoting Lessing himself:

> A philosopher must be very honest to
> avail himself of no poetical or
> rhetorical expedients. (SE, 14)

Or again, in a diatribe against the pretenses of dignity, he says that all things known as dignity are pretenses adopted by the timid of the heart. The genuinely fearless have no need of dignity or ceremonies; they use honesty and straightforward words and bearing as evidence of their self-confident awareness. (D, 136-137) These remarks, and one could cite a great number more, would seem to be the kind of traditional exhortation to truthfulness that one might expect from a philosopher.

Nevertheless, despite these remarks Nietzsche consistently identifies the increase in power with the ability to deceive:

> Increase in 'dissimulation'
> proportionate to the rising order or
> rank of creatures. It seems to be
> lacking in the inorganic world--
> power against power, quite crudely--
> cunning begins in the organic world.
> (WP, 544)

And if it begins there, a thousandfold craftiness belongs to the enhancement, man. Nietzsche does insist that man look at his condition honestly, not hiding behind any form of bad faith. However, as indicated earlier, there is no formal contradiction in Nietzsche between his insistence on honesty and on the use of deception, for he always made clear that the deception was to be known as deception, as interpretation. (See GS, 131, 136)

A recent article has pointed out, too, that the opposition between 'truth' and 'deception' may not be even theoretically clear cut when one considers Nietzsche's reflections on the issue of man in society. The authors correctly maintain that duplicity and contradiction are intrinsic to any role. (11) The nature of a role involves conflict between one's desires and the limitations imposed on these desires by collective life. This is not always immediately apparent, though, for: "The apparent unity of the role reifies this fundamental tension, and hides the tendency toward dispersion and conflict underlying the social order." (12) Roles are instrumental masks of manipulation "while risking contamination by the instrument itself through the habits of its use arising in concerted action over time." (13) In fact, as has been seen, Nietzsche holds that the role and intent may become identical. Accordingly, as the authors of this article rightly point out, the masks are used to distance oneself from the collective and are used as instruments of dominance over the collective. The dual role of mask, then, as of the lie, is to represent fixed demands and movement into uncodified territory. Through the use of masks issues a "dialectic of constructive and destructive, social and anti-social forces." (14)

Frequently, Nietzsche uses the language of masks to urge the independence of the higher types. They ought not seek mass approval: "Rather, go away. Flee into concealment. And have your masks and subtlety, that you maybe mistaken for what you are not, or feared a little." (BGE, 36) The experience of the noble type is conceived by Nietzsche as being beyond comprehension or apprehension by the uninitiated, the unexperienced: "Our doubt as to the communicability of the heart goes deep; solitude not as chosen but as given." (WP, 943, cf. SLFN, 243-244) Masks protect this profundity.

This is, too, the lesson of Zarathustra: words in the marketplace convince no one. On the contrary, words are grossly misunderstood. Peerage is established not through commonality of language, but through mutually similar experience:

> To understand one another, it is
> not enough that one use the same
> words; one also has to use the
> same words for the same species
> of inner experiences; in the end
> one has to have one's experiences
> in common. (BGE, 216)

As Nietzsche remarks in one of his notebooks, in the end one never communicates thoughts per se. One communicates movements, mimic signs, "which we then trace back to thoughts." (WP, 809) Thus, if one lacks the experiential ground of some communication, then one is left in possession of mere signs, without any ability to transfer them or interpret them within a context of personal lived experience. Part of the overman's superiority is precisely his silence, (WP, 921) his readiness and ability to always play a part, (WP, 944), in order to preserve the integrity of his experience and vision even as he walks in the marketplace. When he walks in the marketplace, as happened to Zarathustra, he must appear sometimes ridiculous, for he does not value the lessons of the marketplace. "Men of profound thought appear to themselves in intercourse with others like comedians, for in order to be understood they must always simulate superficiality." (HATH, II, 126)

Indeed, it may even be possible that Nietzsche's writings are designed to conceal something crucial, something that he does not even mention in all his books. This is the judgment of the hermit confronted with a mask:

> The hermit does not believe that any
> philosopher—assuming that every
> philosopher was first of all a
> hermit—ever expressed his real and
> ultimate opinions in books: does
> one not write books precisely to
> conceal what one harbors? Indeed,
> he will doubt whether behind every
> one of his caves there is not, must
> not be, another deeper cave—a more
> comprehensive, stranger, richer world
> beyond the surface, an abysmally
> deep ground behind every ground,
> under every attempt to furnish
> 'grounds'. Every philosophy is
> a foreground philosophy—that is a
> hermit's judgment: "There is
> something arbitrary in his stopping
> here to look back and around, in
> his not digging deeper here but laying
> his spade aside; there is also something
> suspicious about it.' Every philosophy
> also conceals a philosophy,
> every opinion, is also a hideout,
> every word also a mask. (BGE, 229)

The point would seem to be that men of the most profound type are inexhaustible in their richness of experience and intention. Their writings express but part of their depth. Knowing that expression can vulgarize experience, Nietzsche would have us be suspicious of the noble type, since he is probably withholding something from his expressions, indeed, perhaps even something crucial. The

78

hermit is the individual who can clearly examine his motives without the bad faith necessary to relations with others. He can penetrate to the motives of his actions most directly since he need not rely on the mediation of others. The judgment that all philosophy is a foreground philosophy is a hermit's judgment because the hermit can presumably see past all the self-deception of stated motivation. The hermit has lived alone with himself and has presumably penetrated behind all the masks of his own self-deception. Accordingly, he trusts the stated intents of others not at all, particularly those of the superior type, for these both have reason to stand apart from the masses and knows the necessity of masks.

When all is said and done, Nietzsche thinks that life itself is impossible without lies. The lie is a contest on behalf of greater meaning. Lies and masks function first as symbols of power and secondly as means of protection for the possibility of future creation and inner meaning. They both conceal and reveal; in concealing they protect, in revealing they initiate the sufficient meritorious into the 'truths' of the creators. As educational tools, they represent a certain state of mastery, a certain condition of strength. The nature of particular lies or masks and interpretations, depends on experience of one's own power and response to the world. The lie and the mask are necessary for the possibility of life itself, then, since upon that experience depends the possibility of metaphysical horizons of meaning for and of human life. Since there are no genuinely eternal truths, man must function as artist, as liar in order to transfigure his condition in the world. He must create lies which, paradoxically, can be believed. In the end this is to say that the interpretations must be meaningful and therefore true (and not the other way around). In a sense, it might even be said that the greatest lies are necessary for they give the greatest possibility of affirmation. As against this notion of lie, 'Truth' as hypostatized and eternally subsiding would signify the end of meaning. All of this discussion of the lie and the mask, in the end, is no objection to Nietzsche's exhortations to the highest intellectual probity, for he never ascribes an eternal, abiding character to lies, to interpretations. He would have man never forget that an interpretation is, after all, only an interpretation.

Chapter 5

TEACHING THE DANCE

Only in the dance do I know
how to tell the parable of
the highest things.

Nietzsche
(TSZ, 224)

The symbol of the dance occurs frequently in Nietzsche, from the early Birth of Tragedy through the last writings, and the symbol functions in more than a decorative fashion. It is the task of this chapter to show that, in the way 'sight' was the operative symbol for Platonic education, the dance is the symbol of the educational ideal for Nietzsche. The dance is Nietzsche's symbol of a joyous, affirmative appropriation of 'truth' and life. In short, it is a symbol of power which paradoxically is also a form of play. It is to be remembered that in Zarathustra, Nietzsche represents play as the highest activity of a metamorphosed spirit. Play represents the highest unity and capability of man; the dance functions similarly as the symbol of educational success. The dancer is the individual who has brought all his particular masteries into an organized whole, executing a unified artistic creation of life as meaningful.

This last chapter functions as does Nietzsche's dance. I try to unify the various threads of the preceding discussion and embody the efforts of the foregoing pages into a resolution of the problem of education. In what follows here, it will be seen how the dance embodies the contest, how the dance is the grand style which is the meaningful activity Nietzsche so craves, how the dance is related to the discussions of the virtuous danger of the tightrope walker, Nietzsche's own writing style, and how the dance reflects the vision of the eternal return. There is, too, discussion of the remarks that Nietzsche makes with respect to the educational ideal. Moreover, it will be seen, passim, how the dance escapes the charges of educational partialism. The dance is the activity of gods and god-like man. And while in the pages of Nietzsche, the dance functions as an exemplary symbol, when translated into the realm of actual life, the dance becomes the meaning of life itself.

In the first chapter it was maintained that Nietzsche's philosophy was educative in nature. When one looks at the relationship of the symbol of the dance to the remarks he makes on education it is obvious that the dance as a lived practice (as distinct from an intellectual ideal) constitutes one of the exemplary ways in which Nietzsche attempts teaching how to live. This is not to deny, as pointed out before, that intellectual endeavors are necessary; indeed, they are quite necessary states of advancement. However, they are not ends in themselves. If there is anything that gives meaning to life, it is life dancing triumphantly on top of these endeavors. It does not seem necessary to dwell on showing how the dance gives example beyond pointing out that dance is a creative activity which depends upon mastering the various possibilities of movement and blending them into a harmonious whole which is expressive of human meaning. Nietzsche's style of writing is instructive in how to live despite the plethora of philosophical analyses which he gives along the way. The analyses he gives are instructions given with a larger view in mind. The quest for theoretical meaning is ultimately turned into a question of meaning at the level of life itself. The dance symbolizes this exemplary turning of metaphysical and epistemological endeavors towards the question of the meaningful life.

In keeping with his aesthetic perfectionism, Nietzsche holds that certain kinds of individuals were beyond any kind of rational or utilitarian assessment because of the nature of their activity. To them belonged 'grand style' which requires only the felt value on the part of those engaging in that activity. There is a kind of activity which because of its nature seems to be inherently self-validating and meritorious. 'Grand style' requires no justification, apparently, over and above its own practice:

> The highest feelings of power and security
> find expression in that which possesses
> grand style. Power which no longer requires
> proving; which disdains to please, which is
> slow to answer; which is conscious of no
> witnesses around it; which lives oblivious
> of the opposition; which reposes in itself,
> fatalistic, a law among laws: that is what
> speaks of itself in the form of a grand
> style.— (TI, 74)

The dance requires style and expresses power. In exempting grand style from utilitarian measurement, Nietzsche maintains that grand style is not for anything except itself. This, of course, is true of the question of human meaning. The meaning of life is not for anything else. It is its own final cause. When Nietzsche speaks in the quote above of grand style being oblivious to any opposition, he is not repudiating his insistence on the value of the agon, he means only that grand style does not subject itself

82

to the values of opposing styles. Clearly, grand style could not have existed in the first place had it not gone through much opposition. Once having successfully undergone that opposition, it is now beyond the pale of utilitarian measurement, it is meaning unto itself.

It was argued in Chapter 3 that the <u>agon</u> was the central concept of education, that Nietzsche thought that the circumstances of the contest, varied and occurring at many levels, provided the best learning opportunity. It was also seen that asceticism was a powerful instrument of education in that it embodied a kind of existential contest. How, then, can this decidedly martial imagery of the contest (increasingly more violent the more Nietzsche penned) be reconciled with the apparently non-martial imagery of dancing? Can the apparently contradictory images of <u>agon</u> and <u>dance</u> be compatible in educational theory?

It should be evident from the foregoing discussions that the contradiction is only an apparent one. For as indicated earlier, Nietzsche conceived of the contest not as necessarily martial involvement (though that certainly could be a form of contest), but rather as an involvement or antagonism between opposing forces. Alderman point this out thus:

> Nietzsche's own example of a metaphorical
> war is that which takes place in a temple
> between the vault and the arch; through
> their opposition a third, harmonious
> and beautiful thing is produced which
> is the product of their stressed opposition.
> In denying such opposition we also deny
> the sense of appropriate place and
> hierarchy, and it is these two denials
> which rule out the possibility of
> creation. (1)

In this larger sense, the dance is a form of contest, for dancing as an art form certainly requires mastery and coordination of divergent forces. The sense of opposing forces is the tension between constitutive elements. The dance in its origins and practice requires such tension, this tension actually issuing in the ability to perform. Thus, the dance is legitimately considered a contest in the deepest meaning of the term.

Nietzsche conceived of philosophy as essentially geared towards teaching how to live. The dance serves the philosophical task in that it serves as the symbol of integrated, unified and creative life. In the dance, all the particular tensions and efforts of an individual have been transformed into a grand pattern of affirmation. And it is this very activity, this very

83

affirmation which is held by Nietzsche as the meaning of life. He rejects a utilitarian approach to the evaluation of human meaning. Of the highest human activity, he says: "That one does not know how to make use of it perhaps even pertains to greatness..." (TI, 104) The highest activities of the highest human beings are beyond the realm of public utilitarian measurement. The dance would seem to be a candidate for affirmative activity beyond utilitarian measurement. The result of a genuinely philosophical education would seem to be pure creativity of joyous affirmation: he lives best who creates. And the dance and play seem paradigmatic examples of such activity. But, it is to be remembered, Nietzsche cannot specify the nature of this play or dance (due to its personal self-constituting quality), he can only symbolize it. This he does in the image of the dance because the dance incorporates and is predicated upon all the values he espouses. At the level of life, as distinct from the level of imagery, the dance is no longer a symbol but is the meaning of creative human life itself.

For Nietzsche the imagery of dancing is an imagery of power whether applied to gods or man. Dancing implies unity and ability. He who can dance can look at the conditions of existence (seeing there death, meaninglessness, suffering and the like) and not find them objections to existence. Three particular uses of the imagery of dance will be singled out before considering the symbol of the dance in relation to the educational ideal per se. For it is in these three instances, the tightrope walker, the writing style, and the eternal return, that one discovers the elements of the dance which should be reflected in the educational mission: the contest, affirmation, and creativity.

With respect to the first example, on the descent from the mountain into the town, Zarathustra finds himself in a marketplace in which a tightrope walker is about to perform. Yet, in German, the performer is not a walker but a dancer (Seiltanzer). Such a language of dancing beautifully symbolizes Nietzsche's intentions. The dancer is literally dancing above the potential danger posed by his fall. When he does in fact die, Zarathustra will not mock the dancer for falling. He says to the man that since he has made danger his vocation, and "there is nothing contemptible in that." (TSZ, 132) Though the man flirts with death by balancing himself precariously on a rope high above the ground, yet he does not find the danger involved any objection to his activity. In fact, not only does he find no objection, he can still be a dancer! That is to say that he can still affirm the value of his activity, demanding of one, as it does, tremendous exertion and mortal danger. That he was tumbled to the ground in the confusion caused by the appearance of the mocking jester might mean that he had not completely mastered his situation, that he was not yet the master dancer. The jester would represent here both the impediments to the overman and his herald. Zarathustra laments that a jester can

84

become man's fatality, yet it is the jester himself who jibes the rope-dancer: "you block the way for one better than yourself." (TSZ, 131) But in any case, the imagery of dancing here is intimately tied to the concept of power and mastery. For the tightrope dancer is at least master of himself with respect to affirming the value of his activity in the face of its possible perils.

Nietzsche often used the imagery of dancing when referring to his own writing style. He thought of himself, of course, as a master stylist, and the use of the dancing imagery reflects that belief. In a letter to Erwin Rohde, Nietzsche claims that the first book of Zarathustra brings the German language to perfection (after Goethe and Luther) and as if to attest to that claim says further: "My style is a dance—it plays with all sorts of symmetries, only to leap over and scoff at them" (NSP, 78). The use of the dance imagery highlights Nietzsche's intention to say no with a dance. The use of language resembles a large group of interacting desires and possibilities. One dances with them to one's own purpose. Yet even so, one is not bound by one's creation. One remains, like Nietzsche, able to dance away from them to other possibilities.

In a lament on the state of German writing, Nietzsche complains about the "swamps of sound and rhythms that do not dance." (BGE, 182) He laments about the state of prose in that it is not unified, that it does not represent a masterful coordination, that it exhibits detrimental partialisms. For example, he says that Germans write while their "ears are put away in a drawer" (BGE, 183). That is to say that Germans do not give any attention to what their written language sounds like, and thus since they do not have complete mastery, they cannot effect rhythms that dance.

In an article specifically on Nietzsche and the dance, Edward Mooney points out that Nietzsche may have drawn on the Hindu god of dance, Siva Nataraja, in his depiction of a dancing god. He writes that such an influence is possible because Nietzsche's use of dancing recalls an Indian deity:

> In briefest outline, Siva is the
> embodiment of dynamism and energy, the
> motive force behind the ever-changing
> flux of phenomena. He is lord of
> creation and destruction. Through
> dance, he forms, sustains, and breaks
> up the natural world. (2)

While the direct evidence for claiming that Nietzsche was in fact influenced by this Hindu god is hardly conclusive (as Mooney himself points out), certainly as described above, this god Siva

85

would represent an ideal Nietzschean god in that one might might well describe him as a merging of Apollo and Dionysus, the god who both creates and destroys. Alderman calls Dionysus the dancing god and Apollo the god of dreams. (3) While this is certainly fair in a consideration of, say, the Birth of Tragedy, in which Dionysus represents dancing, intoxication, and revelry generally (even the darkest revelry), it should be ke in mind that the distinction is not a completely accurate one. For even dancing presupposes the Apollinian power of ordering. Dancing might be called an intoxicated ordering. One difference to be noted with respect to the Hindu god, though, is rather important. If Siva is the god who forms, sustains and breaks up the natural world, it would be well to keep in mind that for Nietzsche no such world exists. As indicated earlier, the world exists only to the extent that it is formed and interpreted.

Mooney goes on to show how the dance is a lived response to moral dilemmas, rightly stressing Nietzschean insistence on lived experience. As Mooney indicates: "So in the realm of moral obstacles, what counts is sensitive, imaginative gesture, fitted creatively to circumstance." (4) For the dance does not offer rational articulate solutions. Rather it embodies and presupposes them. The dance as a form of creative response is beyond good and evil because it does not fit into the categories offered by traditional moral valuations.

Mooney ties the notion of the dance to the pivotal theme of eternal recurrence. First, he remarks that whether the doctrine is cosmologically intended or tied to the quality of experience, its ultimate meaning is as a test of power, a challenge to create meaning. There are, too, parallels between dance and eternal recurrence. Like the eternal recurrence, in the dance there are no transcendent beginnings or endings, "its steps recur endlessly" (5). This is not to say that when Nietzsche describes the eternal return in dance-like language he imputes any intentionality behind the patterns of the universe. Nietzsche removes all purposefulness from the world except that of human intentionality. The meaning of the world is the meaning one might ascribe to it. The eternal return as dance, I take it, reinforces Nietzsche's vision of dancing man in dancing world. That a step in a dance is repeated is likewise no refutation of its value. That the world recurs is no refutation of the world.

Mooney shows how the eternal recurrence functions as a test of human affirmation. He says:

> Imagine a child facing a life of dance.
> Gazing on the prospect of years of
> practice, years of thankless routine,
> with no guarantee of success or reward,
> should a child not despair? Could a

> man sustain a commitment to the promise
> of life, become joyful and exuberant,
> knowing that his every moment of pain
> and pleasure alike, would be repeated
> endlessly as the steps of an eternal
> dance, without hope of final peace or
> resolution? The idea of eternal
> recurrence served as a clinical test
> for pessimism, a test of man's
> commitment to life. (6)

Indeed, if the task of achieving some sort of mastery is so apparently difficult how much more difficult is achieving mastery of an image of the universe which posits no final purpose, but that endlessly and meaninglessly repeats itself! But if one views the eternal return as itself a kind of cosmic dance, as its patterns repeat themselves endlessly in time, then one does not look for a final purpose over and above the dance. The dance is itself the meaning. Of course, as Mooney points out, Nietzsche did not think that all or perhaps even most individuals would be able to accept such a meaning, since individuals exist at different levels of power. But then again, neither can all individuals dance in the same way. The acceptance of the meaning of the eternal return signifies the acceptance of a kind of cosmic dance. To appreciate this dance, one must be prepared to impart to the world one's own meaning through personal creativity.

What is the particular relation of the dance to the educational ideal? It has been argued all along that the educational ideal and the philosophical ideal meet in one, that they are identical since the task of philosophy is to inaugurate experiments of human living, and education is the praxis of initiation such experiments. The remarks that Nietzsche makes on this account show that this contention is more than simply an imposed reading. To begin with one example which serves the point as well as many others could, Nietzsche scores the English for their perceived lacks. This, of course, he did many a time, but in Beyond Good and Evil, he uses precisely the language of music and dancing:

> But what is offensive even in the most
> humane Englishman is his lack of music,
> speaking metaphorically (but not only
> metaphorically): in the movements of
> his soul and body he has no rhythm and
> dance, indeed not even the desire for
> rhythm and dance, for 'music' (BGE, 190).

Nietzsche's criticism of a failure in living is here expressed with reference to a paradigm of dancing, a paradigm of unity in creative expression. Nietzsche thought of the dance as a test and expression of mastery. The English evidently do not meet such a test, to his way of thinking. Whether that is true or not, the criterion is as important as what it judges. The dance is the test of the experimental interpretation of life. "Does it dance?" is the question Nietzsche might ask in regard to the legitimacy of a particular lived interpretation of existence. For if it dances, then it creates, and thus affirms. And if it does not dance, then it is not yet an avenue to mastery of human meaning.

The text Zarathustra gives an indication how Nietzsche turns Zarathustra himself into a dancer. As pointed out by Alderman, after the thought of the eternal return has been articulated, endured and overcome by Zarathustra, the following sections describe his discovery of the dance, of embodied music. In the "Second Dance Song" he actually dances, he is no longer a dance critic. (7)

When presenting not only the theoretical Zarathustra but also when discussing the needs of the university students of his day, Nietzsche insisted again and again on the dance. In Twilight, he reiterates his objection to German writing:

> Read German books: no longer the
> remotest recollection that a
> technique, a plan of instruction,
> a will to mastery is required for
> thinking--that thing has to be
> learned in the way dancing has to
> be learned, as a form of dancing.
> (TI, 65)

The inability to dance that haunts German prose, haunts university education as well. Education ought to promote intellectual light feet and nuance, but as indicated in the second chapter, Nietzsche found time and again forms of partialism that disallowed the possibility of such attributes. He indicates explicitly the form education must take:

> For dancing in any form cannot be
> divorced from a noble education,
> being able to dance with the feet,
> with concepts, with words: do I
> still have to say that one has to be
> able to dance with the pen--that
> writing has to be learned? (TI, 66)

German universities fail to teach dancing for a number of reasons: they are democratic, they have no instructional unity, they are predicated upon decadent values, and they hold up false models of achievement. All these things Nietzsche finds destructive of dancing as the human ideal. And since educational systems cannot achieve this ideal, then clearly they are philosophical failures as well. As the situation stood, Nietzsche thought that the cultural conditions precluded any possibility of dancing issuing from the universities or from society at large for that matter. Hence his flight from schools and the masses to the solitude where creativity and living are identical.

Nietzsche knew that to effect the kind of changes he envisioned, the whole range of social practices and their foundational values would have to be changed. Plato knew this quite well, too. He, for example, attempted to control all music and even play by the dictates of reason. The control of music and poetry in the Republic is well known. Plato thought that music, poetry, and dancing influenced the course of the soul's development such that the philosopher kings must control them in order to dispose the populace to the virtues of reason and moral probity. In the Laws, Plato sets down regulations that control play and dancing, using 'Egyptian' methods, that is, by basing regulations on conformity with the wishes of the gods. (8) Even if the Laws is intended as a more practical guide to ruling than the Republic is generally considered, still Plato dwells on the control of all the elements necessary to produce a citizenry disposed to virtue and the life of reason. He opposes all innovation for innovation's sake, calling it "the biggest menace that can ever afflict a state." (9) Far from desiring creativity, Plato wanted the social order to reflect as far as possible the eternal world of reason. Towards this end he suggested the following regulatory practices:

> I maintain that no one in any state
> has grasped that children's games
> affect legislation so crucially as to
> determine whether the laws that are
> passed will survive or not. If you
> control the way children play, and the
> same children always play the same games
> under the same rules and in the same
> conditions, and get pleasure from the
> same toys, you'll find that the
> conventions of adult life too are left
> in peace without alteration. (10)

In his attempt to shape a citizenry from their childhood (and even before: he gives instructions to mothers on how to treat their children while yet unborn!), he goes on to regulate the kinds of dancing that are permissible. He makes this distinction: "Two varieties, the decent and the disreputable." (11) The real distinction, of course, hinges on whether or not these dances can be put to use in the overall moral order of the state. Plato specifically excludes the Bacchic dances since they resist all attempts at classification since it is so hard to determine what their purpose is. The state should concern itself with and promote dances which are concerned with war and peace. (12)

Given his radically different metaphysics, Plato could not but draw different conclusions about the status of dancing and music than did Nietzsche. The former saw them as instruments to be controlled on behalf of advancing the cause of reason, while the latter saw them as the desirable symbols of human powers, ends in themselves requiring no utilitarian assessment. In opposition to Plato, however, Nietzsche did not want to identify reason as the highest human activity. For him, the need for truth at the theoretical level reflected a lack of meaning at the level of lived experience. He thought that by holding play and dancing as symbols of the highest human activity he could restore meaning to humanity since these activities did not presume, indeed could not function under any divorce between thought and action, a divorce theoretical speculation required. Accordingly, he could not restrict as Plato did, the character of dance and playing. He could indicate the values which would enlarge the possibility of the highest forms and greatest horizons of dancing and playing. This he did in his attempt to revaluate all values. But the ultimate intent was to liberate playing and dancing from the strictures into which Plato and even current regimes attempt to imposes them such that they can display, as the gestures that they are, the meaning of human existence.

The dance has two other features which recommend it to Nietzsche's advocacy of certain human values. On the one hand, dancing escapes the theoretical charge of educational partialism, and also contains the element of revealing and concealing which relates it to the notion of mask and lie. The dance educates the whole person. One cannot teach someone to dance by training only the arms, say, or the legs; one educates a dancer, not any of his or her particular parts. By holding the dance as the educational ideal, therefore, Nietzsche is proposing that culture should educate persons in toto. An education, properly speaking, trains, informs, and generates whole persons, not the kind of students Nietzsche saw emerging from the institutions of his day, students warped to the demands of scientism, technicism, or Statism. The latter kind of education gives birth to 'inverse cripples,' that is, persons who have been developed in only one aspect to the exclusion of all their other talents. Recalling the opening of Schopenhauer as Educator, it is clear that Nietzsche thought that education should not develop merely some talents, but all those elements which compose both the center and periphery of an individual. The dance quite adequately and beautifully symbolizes this concern; for a student of the dance cannot develop some part of his/her body to the exclusion of the others. Education must be thorough and of the whole person.

While the notion of the dance does not completely

90

correspond to the discussion of the use of masks and lies in Nietzsche, it does have resemblance in that with respect to understanding the meaning of the dance, issues of revealing and concealing are raised. For in performance the dancer is essentially standing on the practice and training which has preceded the performance. Yet the effort must be concealed, i.e., not forthrightly evident as the mechanical precedent of the action, else the dance is stilted, awkward, a failure. Rather the effort is concealed in the flawless execution of the dance. Yet at the same time the strength, endurance and magnitude of the performance is revealed to those initiates who understand the dynamics of each movement, of the training and mastery required for each supple revelatory movement. The dance, then, depends upon the notions of revealing and concealing that were outlined as instrumental in Nietzsche's conceptual plan of the relationship between teacher and student, between tyro and the initiated one.

It should be noted in passing, too, that Nietzsche even applies the imagery of dancing to culture. What applies to the individual applies as well to a whole culture: the divergent strains of the culture are brought together into a unified, creative whole. Nietzsche says: "it may be remembered that dancing is not the same as a dull reeling to and fro between different impulses. High culture will resemble a bold dance,—wherefore, as has been said, there is need of much strength and suppleness." (HATH, I, 256) Though he would not and could not specify the exact nature of the form of society's way of conduct, Nietzsche at least attempted to express his vision through the imagery of the dance.

The notion of the dance, beyond its relation with education and culture also shares the status of meaningful, creative play since the dance can be understood as a form of play. It would seem that for Nietzsche, dancing is a form of play in that both impose structures of meaning on the realm of experience without imputing necessity to those interpretations. Plato, possessed of idealist standards of truth wanted to make play and dancing serve those standards. Nietzsche, by contrast, located in creative, dynamic activity the source of the highest human meaning. (see TSZ, 137-140) Thus it would seem that dancing and playing are not only symbols of human meaning, in lived experience they are actually constitutive of meaning. The dance or playing becomes the meaning of existence because of their capacity for subjective (that is, belonging to a subject) meaning-constitution. Nietzsche insists that the superior type is the one who overflows with power. Yet he also ranks the child as the highest metamorphosis of the spirit. According to the representation in Zarathustra, "The child is innocence and forgetting, a new beginning, a game, a self-propelled wheel, a first movement, a sacred 'Yes'" (TSZ, 139). The noble human being, then, is like the child who plays with the world, giving it first this meaning,

91

next that. And because there is no eternal criterion against which to measure these interpretations, only the internal criterion of individual power, then there is no objection to such a child's play. Nietzsche says in approbation:

> 'Play,' the useless—as the ideal
> of him who is overfull of strength,
> as 'childlike.' The childlikeness
> of God, pais paizon. (WP, 797)

Or again:

> I do not know any other way of
> associating with great tasks than
> play: as a sign of greatness
> this is an essential presupposition.
> (EH, 258)

Thus, for all his insistence on the language of power, of martial metaphors, and vitriolic criticism, for Nietzsche, the man of power is the person who plays with the world. But this playing is an excellent playing, it is playing masterfully. It is effecting a dance while writing, while teaching, while living.

The dance is a well-chosen symbol. As a matter of body and spirit, as a matter of willing and being, the dance exemplifies the kind of meaningful life that as the human task Nietzsche held up as the highest philosophical task. The philosopher as educator is an example, is a dancer to the extent that he embodies the lived quest for meaning, meaning which neither fears the darkness of the night nor the metaphysical darkness of absurdity. As dancer, man is faithful to the earth and faithful to his will: he is neither material clod nor incorporeal spirit. When the dance is one's own, when one has light feet, the dance is no longer symbol, it is constitutive of meaning.

In The Birth of Tragedy, Nietzsche announced art as the highest metaphysical activity. It seems to me that this claim must mean that artistry is the mode of understanding being, that is, one endows being with meaning. Artistry brought home to reside in one's life is the dance. All dances are not of equal value, for Nietzsche, to be sure. But neither can there be a universally prescribed dance. As a matter of will, the artistic task is genuinely each person's own. For Nietzsche, when all is well with man, when philosophy and education succeed in the constitution of meaningful life, there is no distinction, in the haunting language of Yeats, between the dancer and the dance.

> Whoever is a teacher through
> and through takes all things
> seriously in relation to his
> students--even himself.
>
> Nietzsche
> (BGE, 79)

Nietzsche's concern with education flowed from his larger moral concerns. How can one teach man to live? How can man know the value of the conquest of resentment, of pity? Professor Nietzsche outlined his earliest concerns with these questions in an unfinished and abandoned series of lectures at Basel. But his larger thematic issues are the true battleground of his contributions to man and education. Nietzsche thought that the rescue of philosophy as a genuine lived discipline would come through its escape from the confines of academe. The rehabilitation of education might be possible only in a similar fashion. Hopefully, what has been done in this book is a gathering of the various threads pertinent to the subject of education, and unifying them into some sort of fabric which does justice to Nietzsche's overall concerns.

If one considers the institution, the process, and the product of education as the three guiding foci in the subject of educational philosophy, then it can be seen that Nietzsche was not amiss in addressing them all. Chapter 2, Nietzsche on University Education, addresses Nietzsche's reaction to and assessment of the institutions of education. Chapter 3, The Contest and Education, and Chapter 4, The Teacher and the Lie, address the process of education proposed by Nietzsche, the agon. Chapter 5, Teaching the Dance, attempts a reflection on the product of education, the dancer. Of course, these three issues do not exhaust the category of education, but they do form the basic framework of discussion about education.

Chapter 1, The Character of Philosophy, showed that no interpreter of Nietzsche makes much of Nietzsche's educational philosophizing although his own remarks certainly make the link between philosophy and education clear. As was seen, while Nietzsche's concerns in metaphysics, morals, and reflections on language have placed him in the rank of the philosophers, he himself thought that philosophy had a larger task than any of the isolated philosophical labors. Nietzsche was fond of pointing out that he had to have been a scholar for a time else he would not have known or been able to shed its ideals. (See, for example, EH, 282.) The endeavors of philosophers with metaphysics, logic and the rest, too, were necessary stages of the development of man. But they must be denied eventually because life demands it (cf. ADHL, 22). The task of philosophy lies beyond criticism, beyond mere metaphysics. Philosophy must educate, must show man lived examples of how to live. And this education must heighten life, not reinforce the already evident failures of current education (see, for example the content versus form discussion in ADHL, 25 ff.) To be sure, this education, while aiming at the whole of mankind is specifically focussed on the possibility of the overman as willed in particular.

The range of Nietzsche's concern with education spans all his books and all his stages of writing. The explicit concerns that characterize Nietzsche's objections to the theory and practice of university education as he knew it, are to be understood in the context of their failure to comply with the philosophical task outlined in Chapter 1. Current schools and cultural institutions foster educational partialism in that they simply process human beings for their adequate participation in existing social compacts. Consequently, they do not educate in the etymological sense of 'leading out.' Genuine philosophy, and therefore genuine education, Nietzsche thinks, ends in transforming action/living, not in professorialism or technicism, for these latter are species of partialism which prevent genuine fruition of human beings. The rescue of education implies a liberation of philosophy and educational institutions, from the elements which inform current practice. Of course, Nietzsche rejects the metaphysics which forms the conceptual foundation of the university's architecture of knowledge. Moreover, he singled out the lack of solitude, the democratization of the schools and the failure of education to quicken life as serious shortcomings. The countermovement he envisioned is contained in his ethic of amor fati, an ethic of endless, striving creativity and self-overcoming. Not scholarship but experience in life would teach man the way of heightened vitality.

And if experience is the crux of the educational enterprise, then Nietzsche consistently advocated, both implicitly and explicitly, the contest as the true form of education. Chapter 3 reviewed Nietzsche's inexorably agonal conception of education. The contest is the test and measure of human power. It provides the touchstone of accomplishment and the spur to higher creativity. The contest is not merely the intellectual contest, the contest, say of disinterested dialectic. Rather, Nietzsche saw the contest as valuable at every level of human life. His Thus Spoke Zarathustra reveals the sage Zarathustra in a continuing struggle with himself, with others, with the world itself. And true to his position on various lived interpretations of the world, Nietzsche could not ask for followers strictly speaking. The ultimate advice of the teacher must be: "This is my way, where is yours?" (TSZ, 307) The process of education is experiential struggle at all facets of human life.

If the contest is the form or the process of education, then the masks and lies that Nietzsche so often mentions (and does not mention) are to be understood as facets of the experiential struggle of education. Nietzsche ascribes the right to lie to the teacher as an instrument of the agon, silence and aphorisms being among the chief masks Nietzsche himself uses. The educator must make use of these in order to initiate the student into the rigors of the contest and to preserve his own self from those who could not understand him. And while Nietzsche does criticize the use of lies by others, it was pointed out that he did not object to the lie itself (indeed, he points out that no one objects to something merely because of its falsity) but he objected to the decadent ends those lies served, Christian religion, for example. The lie is an integral part of life, it serves as a horizon of meaning: "Every living thing needs to be surrounded by an atmosphere, a mysterious circle of mist: if one robs it of this veil, if one condemns a religion, an art, a genius to orbit as a star without an atmosphere: then one should not wonder about its rapidly becoming withered, hard and barren." (ADHL, 40) And, as was discussed, this necessary masking of the horizons of life often takes the form of lies. For the creator often seems to speak in lies by virtue of the novelty of what he is saying. The lie and the mask, then, are desirable components of the contest which enlightens.

Finally, seeing the contest embedded at all levels of human life, one is in a position to look at how Nietzsche symbolized the issue of this contest. Chapter 5 discussed how Nietzsche's often violent language issues in the imagery of the dance. For Nietzsche, not scholarship, not science, not service to the state but the dance represents genuine education. The dance is the symbol of joyous, cheerful, and creatively masterful existence. Dance combines with playing and thereby reflects Nietzsche's conception of the highest will to power. The dance as a lived practice is the meaning of life. The exercise of metaphysics, logic, and epistemology are necessary endeavors, philosophical endeavors which allow one to engage in masterful, informed dance. The dance presumes and expresses power. Its style is beyond any utilitarian measurement. The wide-ranging uses of the symbol always imply unity and ability,but especially cheerfulness in the face of existence. Thus it is that Nietzsche would teach men to dance even as the cosmos is engaged in the dance of the eternal return. The aim of philosophy and education, therefore, may be said to be the dance insofar as it reflects the highest level of human power which is itself the meaning of the earth.

Nietzsche uses the following epigram as the opening to Beyond Good and Evil, Prelude to a Philosophy of the Future. This litany against dogmatism in all its forms, but most especially against philosophical dogmatism guides Nietzsche's hand as it touches and illuminates problem after problem:

> Supposing truth is a woman—what then?
> Are there not grounds for the suspicion
> that all philosophers, insofar as they
> were dogmatists, have been very inexpert
> about women? That the gruesome seriousness,
> the clumsy obtrusiveness with which they
> have usually approached truth so far
> have been awkward and very improper
> methods for winning a woman's heart?
> What is certain is that she has not
> allowed herself to be won and today every
> kind of dogmatism is left standing
> dispirited and discouraged. If it is
> left standing at all! For there are
> scoffers who claim that it has fallen,
> that all dogmatism lies on the ground—
> even more, that all dogmatism is dying.
> (BGE, 2)

One would be well advised to use this as a guiding image in reading the man who penned it.

Nietzsche is a dancing thinker, a profound thinker, an impassioned thinker. His passion is relentless. Such a constellation of traits ought to itself forwarn of a writer who merits special pains, whose writing admits of a wide breadth of interest and interpretation. When confronted with a thinker who actively advocates that man become creative, that he generates his own interpretations of the world, the reader is aware that here is a writer who must be seduced in order to reveal his secret, who will not surrender his secret to the casual glance.

The reader's own interests and intellectual dispositions will color any reading of Nietzsche. As Nietzsche himself pointed out: "Ultimately, nobody can get more out of things, including books, than he already knows. For what one lacks access to from experience one will have no ear." (EH, 261) A reading of Nietzsche in a particular way will finally be a strange blend of Nietzsche's clearly stated opinions, his rich allusions, interpretations of his symbolism, the reader's interests, and the reader's methodology. If one is to be a 'true' reader of Nietzsche, one must respond, too, with the commitment of one's own life to one's own life.

In the foregoing argument, I hope that I have not ridden too roughshod over Nietzsche's 'truth,' that I have been a somewhat adept seducer, listening to Nietzsche before I speak in turn. My suggestion has been to read Nietzsche with an eye keyed in on his interest in education, to see him as from beginning to end concerned with the role of experience in education of man in the art of living. His biography and writing style provide much evidence for insisting on such an educational concern. At the beginning of his university career, Nietzsche actively sought out a university chair in philosophy, claiming his interest in educational questions as a credential. In the retrospective Ecce Homo, he began his list of accomplishments by claiming that with respect to decadence and the possibility of a new beginning, he was the teacher par excellence (EH, 222). Throughout his lifetime, he never forgot the university life he had to leave. He never forgot its most egregious errors. And though he never completely devoted himself to a formal, sustained treatise on education, he did write the magisterial Zarathustra, and all his other works illuminate the subject of education in one way or another.

Whether Nietzsche is a philosopher is no longer a reputable question. The philosophical question he poses is our question, the question of meaning. And he has posed it in the most demanding of ways. His answers will not be our answers, but neither should they be: "One repays a teacher badly if one remains nothing but a pupil." (TSZ, 190) The testimony of Nietzsche's life, independent of his works, shows, I think, the ardor of humanness that abided in him. When one adds his writings to that testimony, one might be tempted to call him holy unless he had not himself disowned that designation. One can compliment him though by judging him by his own criterion, that by which he judged Schopenhauer as educator: what ideal has he set above us? Nietzsche as educator has shown us the ideal of self-generated, meaningful life. That ideal is indeed far, far above us. Between nothingness and the nothingness of the future, there is, for Nietzsche, only life, which is at once the most fragile, the most beautiful, and the most meaningful of all existing things.

In the citations that follow, reference is made to author and page. For full citation, refer to the Bibliography.

Introduction

1. All quotes from Nietzsche are cited in the text, indicating original source and page number. Key to the abbreviations and the specific texts will be found at the beginning of the bibliography. For example, this quote is from Selected Letters of Friedrich Nietzsche, p. 227.

2. The following authors (complete reference is in the Bibliography) make no mention of Nietzsche: Luella Cole, James Mulhern, Henry J. Perkinson, Edward J. Power, Kingsley Price. Robert Rusk mentions Nietzsche only for his comments on Christianity. James L. Jarrett mentions Nietzsche but only in a very peripheral way. Finally, John S. Brubacher mentions that Nietzsche had little impact on education but is instructive in the aristocratic drift of his times. To wit, Brubacher mentions The Future of Our Educational Institutions, although he ties the ideas of that book to Darwinism, a doctrine that Nietzsche clearly repudiated.

In Education and the Endangered Individual, Brian V. Hill discusses Nietzsche with respect to educational concerns. Looking to determine the standing of the individual to be educated, Hill concludes that "It is apparent that the human individual as such is afforded neither respect nor protection in the society of Nietzsche's dreams." (p. 57) Hill uses a biological, species-based interpretation of the overman to show that Nietzsche himself is governed by an increasingly militaristic, Napoleonic warlord image: "One must wonder whether even the yea-saying Superman of Thus Spoke Zarathustra has not been swallowed up by the monsters of militarism and barbarism." (p. 57) Hill states that in Nietzsche's view "the individual possesses no intrinsic worth." (p. 58)

One can respond to this criticism in a number of ways. The most important criticism is that, from a Nietzschean point of view, Hill wrongly makes the 'superman' a matter of species evolution. Secondly, it seems to me that he substantially overstates the possible barbarism following from Nietzsche's remarks. The domination of the masses can be as much a matter of meaning as militarism. Lastly, Nietzsche could characterize Hill's criticisms as expressions of the very nihilism and decadence to be resisted. Hill's ultimate battle with Nietzsche must be a matter of metaphysical models of man, not merely a matter of rejecting radical aristocratism because it might entail "slavery in every sense, including the power to maim and exterminate." (p. 58)

   Finally, the preliminary spadework for this book was done in 1980, at which time I found, in English, an article by Laurence Lampert which treated Nietzsche as a teacher. Subsequently, Harold Alderman's Nietzsche's Gift appeared.   I comment on both these authors at the end of Chapter III.

Chapter 1: The Character of Philosophy

1. John Keats, letter to J.H. Reynold, 3 May 1818.
2. Heidegger, p. 4.
3. Heidegger, p. 9.
4. Howey, p. 9.
5. Heidegger, p. 4.
6. Heidegger, p. 4.
7. Heidegger, p. 4.
8. Cf. Howey.
9. Kaufmann, Nietzsche, p. 79.
10. Kaufmann, Nietzsche, p. 86.
11. Kaufmann, Nietzsche, p. 90.
12. Kaufmann, Nietzsche, p. 90.
13. Kaufmann, Nietzsche, p. 94.
14. Kaufmann, Nietzsche, p. 80.
15. Danto, p. 12.
16. Danto, p. 12.
17. Danto, p. 12.
18. Danto, p. 13.
19. Danto, p. 13.
20. Danto, p. 13.
21. Copleston, pp. 226-238.
22. Copleston, p. 235.
23. I refer the reader to the selections by Grimm, with whose conclusions I am largely in agreement.
24. Copleston, p. 222-223.
25. Copleston, p. 224.
26. Alderman, p. 1.
27. Alderman, p. 2.
28. Alderman, p. 137.
29. Alderman, p. 160.
30. Alderman, p. 138.
31. Alderman, p. 113.
32. Alderman, p. 6.
33. Books are not ends in themselves. Good style takes a reader beyond the book to an encounter with his own and the writer's subjectivity.   "Everything in Nietzsche's writing exemplifies these two insights, and they must be kept in mind as a constant set of reminders." "Nietzsche's method then is a poetic fictive one which by de-emphasizing the idea of the book-in-itself emphasizes the reality of the reader and his dialogical response to the subtext." Alderman, p. 14.
34. Alderman, p. 6.

35. Alderman, p. 13.
36. Deighton, p. viii.
37. Burgess, p. 258.
38. Alderman, p. 113.
39. Kaufmann, Discovering, p. 5.
40. Sartre, p. 158.
41. Kaufmann, Discovering, p. 42.

Chapter 2: Nietzsche on University Education

1. Sartre, p. 23.

Chapter 3: The Contest and Education

1. Sartre, p. 43.
2. Barrett, p. 199.
3. In "Nazism as a Nietzschean 'Experiment'," K.R. Fischer attempts to show that Nietzsche, though not an accessory per se, was certainly a precursor to Nazism. His argument rests on the contentions that Nietzsche was first and foremost concerned with lived experiment, and the ambiguity of such remarks as "what is falling, push," or "all truths are soaked in blood." (Fischer, p. 33) Both of these points are conceded. Yet for every violent remark in Nietzsche, there is one that can be construed in opposition to Nazism. The retreat of Zarathustra from the world of followers, for example, can be counted as testimony to the path the overman must go. In other places, Nietzsche says that he does not want violence against the masses, for that is unworthy of the genuine philosopher. (WP, 893, 894) But then again, he does remark that war is to be declared against the masses. (WP, 861) To claim that Nietzsche is a precursor to Nazism is merely to assert that there are apparent ideological resemblances between the two. That being the case, the term precursor is much too vague since by that reckoning even Greek and Roman philosophers preached the same virtues extolled by Hitler and Nietzsche, which makes them, apparently, precursors to Nazism. As Fischer says, the texts are ambiguous, why then draw so strong a conclusion?
4. Nietzsche's deification of man is nowhere more evident, in my opinion, than in his proof for the non-existence of god(s): "If there were gods how could I bear not to be a god? Hence, there are no gods." (TSZ, 198) By all logical accounts this argument is a complete failure. But by Nietzsche's criterion of lived power, it is most true. It is true since it most expands the possibility for man, to the point of putting man at the center of the universe, metaphysically if not topographically.
5. Robert C. Solomon has written a book which I will recommend rather then recount. The Passions strikes a resonantly Nietzschean tone in discussing the problem of reason as against emotion in the prospect of meaningful life.

6. Nietzsche specifically links teaching to the infliction of unhappiness: "As a great educator, one would have to scourge such a race of 'blessed people' mercilessly into unhappiness." (WP, 911)

7. See Lampert.

8. Lampert, p. 312.

9. Lampert, p. 312.

10. Lampert, p. 313.

11. Lampert, p. 330.

12. Lampert, p. 332.

13. Lampert, p. 333.

14. Alderman, p. 31.

15. Alderman, p. 38.

16. In one of his letters, Nietzsche says: "I've been dictating almost every day for two or three hours. But my 'philosophy' — if I have the right to call what tortures me to the very roots of my being by that name — is no longer communicable, at least not by means of print." (NSP, 87)

17. Alderman, pp. 86-87.

18. Valadier, p. 254..

19. Alderman, p. 123.

20. Alderman, p. 124.

21. Alderman, p. 134.

22. One finds these remarks in his books and in his letters. Some selected remarks follow. From Zarathustra there are these paradigmatic remarks which capsulize the spirit and the letter of that book: "One repays a teacher badly if one always remains nothing but a pupil. And why do you not want to pluck at my wreath?" (TSZ, 190) "This is my way, where is yours?" (TSZ, 307) From another work: "Whoever secedes from us offends not us, perhaps, but certainly our adherents." (HATH, II, 169) "To Live as Far as Possible Without a Following.--How small is the importance of followers when we first grasp when we have ceased to be the followers of our followers." (HATH, II, 168) From the letters: "Followers, I do not want. May each man, or woman,become his or her true disciple." (NUL, 77) "Now I have shaken off what is extraneous to me: people, friends and enemies, habits, comforts, books; I live in solitude--years of it, if needs be--until once more, ripened and complete as a philosopher of life, I may associate with people (and then probably be obliged to do so). Can you remain, in spite of everything, as kindly disposed to me as you were--or, rather, will you be able to do so? You can see that I have become so candid that I can endure only human relationships which are absolutely genuine. I avoid half-friendships and especially partisan associations; I want no adherents. May every man (and woman) be his own adherent only." (SLFN, 168) "It is by no means necessary, in fact, not even desirable, that you take my side. On the contrary, I'd regard a good measure of curiosity, as if one were confronting a foreign growth with some ironical resistance, as an incomparably more intelligent attitude toward me..." (NSP, 122) "Also we do not

wish to convert others to our way of thinking, because we feel the gulf between them and ourselves to be one established by nature. Pity becomes truly a familiar feeling to us. We grow more and more silent—there are days on which I do not speak at all except in the service of my work." (SLFN, 64) "Admittedly, others might perish by using the same remedies; that is why I exert everything in warning others against me. Especially this latest book, which is called Die froliche Wissenschaft, will scare many people away from me." (SLFN, 187)

One can explain some of these remarks, of course, in the context of Nietzsche's biography. For example, he was urging in the example taken from NUL, 77 that Lou Salome not fear any domination of her own personality. On the other hand, given the form of his book Zarathustra, one can only conclude that this repudiation and surpassing is an integral part of Nietzsche's thinking, not merely an attempt to explain his own lack of influence. The matter is not reducible to biography.

23. Kaufmann, Nietzsche, pp. 68–69.

24. See, for example, Hollingdale, p. 305, and H.F. Peters, pp. 173–174.

25. For remarks on the possibilities of human life given such a liberation, see EH, 290, 309; TI, 46; D, 228–229. This is by no means a comprehensive listing, though these are highly typical examples. The whole of Zarathustra might be said to be a single exhortation to creativity.

26. The resolution of whether or not Nietzsche's propositions are metaphysical truths deserves far more attention than can be given in a sketch of the issues pertinent to considering Nietzsche as educator. Suffice it to say, though, that I do not think Nietzsche's 'metaphysics' is performatively inconsistent. That is, in the ultimate meaning of his descriptions, he commits no logical error about their status as interpretations. I am in agreement with Grimm about this. There may, however, be a functional primacy of his claims that can render Nietzsche susceptible to claims of contradiction.

Chapter 4: The Teacher and the Lie

1. Don Juan, Canto xi, xxxvii.
2. Kaufmann, Discovering, p. 141.
3. Kaufmann, Discovering, p. 148.
4. Kaufmann, Discovering, p. 151 ff.
5. Of course, Nietzsche does not let women escape any opportunity for a caustic remark at their expense. On the subject of using masks, he says: "There are women who, whenever one examines them, have no inside, but are mere masks. A man is to be pitied who has connection with such almost spectre-like and necessarily unsatisfactory creatures, but it is precisely such women who know how to excite a man's desire most strongly; he seeks for their soul, and seeks, evermore." (HATH, I, 300) Women

are empty masks; the attempt to unmask them is unfruitful for there is, according to this biting misogynist, nothing there. Such a remark is, of course, hardly important to Nietzsche's theory of masks, though it does indicate the essential response to a mask or a lie, namely the attempt to find what is behind it.

6. Alderman, p. 9.
7. Alderman, p. 11.
8. Kaplan and Weiglus, p. 302.
9. Bok, p. 214 ff.
10. Bok, p. 130 ff.
11. Kaplan and Weiglus, p. 292.
12. Kaplan and Weiglus, p. 292.
13. Kaplan and Weiglus, p. 292.
14. Kaplan and Weiglus, p. 295.

Chapter 5: Teaching the Dance

1. Alderman, p. 53.
2. Mooney, p. 39.
3. Alderman, p. 139.
4. Mooney, p. 40.
5. Mooney, p. 41.
6. Mooney, p. 42.
7. Alderman, p. 102.
8. Plato, Laws, 799b.
9. Plato, Laws, 797c.
10. Plato, Laws, 797a-b.
11. Plato, Laws, 814e.
12. Plato, Laws, 814d-815d.

Following is a list of works by Nietzsche referred to the in text. Abbreviation in the left-hand column indicates how the works are identified in the references. A completely bibliography of all other works referred to in the text follows this listing.

Works by Nietzsche

AC   The AntiChrist. R.J. Hollingdale, trans. Great
        Britain: Penguin Books, 1968.

ADHL   On the Advantage and Disadvantage of History
        for Life. Peter Preuss, trans. Indianapolis,
        Cambridge: Hackett Publishing Company, 1980.

BGE   Beyond Good and Evil. Walter Kaufmann, trans.
        New: York, Vintage Books, 1966.

BT   The Birth of Tragedy. Walter Kaufmann, trans.
        New York, Vintage Books, 1977.

D   Daybreak: Thoughts on the Prejudices of
        Morality. R.J. Hollingdale, trans. Cambridge:
        Cambridge University Press, 1982.

EH   Ecce Homo. Walter Kaufmann, trans. New York:
        Vintage Books, 1967.

FEI   On the Future of Our Educational Institutions.
        In The Complete Works of Friedrich Nietzsche.
        Vol. 3. Oscar Levy, ed. J.M. Kennedy, trans.
        New York: Russell and Russell, 1964.

GM   On the Genealogy of Morals. Walter Kaufmann,
        trans. New York: Vintage Books, 1974.

HATH   Human, All-Too-Human. In The Complete Works of
        Friedrich Nietzsche. Vols. 6 (I) and 7 (II).
        Oscar Levy, ed., Paul Cohn, trans. New York:
        Russell and Russell, 1964.

PN   The Portable Nietzsche. Walter Kaufmann, trans.
        and ed. New York: Vintage Books, 1968.

PT   Philosophy and Truth, Selections from Nietzsche's
        Notebooks of the Early 1870's. Daniel Breazeale,
        trans. and ed. New Jersey, Humanities Press;
        Sussex, Harvester Press, 1979.

SE   Schopenhauer as Educator. J.W. Hillesheim and M.R.
Simpson, trans. South Bend, Indiana: Gateway
Editions, Ltd., 1965.

TI   Twilight of the Idols. R.J. Hollingdale, trans.
Great Britain, Penguin Books, 1965.

TSZ   Thus Spoke Zarathustra in The Portable Nietzsche.
Walter Kaufmann, ed and trans. New York: The
Viking Press, 1954, 1968.

WP   The Will to Power. Walter Kaufmann, ed., Walter
Kaufmann and R.J. Hollingdale, trans. New York:
Vintage Books, 1967.

Letters

NSP   Nietzsche: A Self-Portrait from his Letters.
Peter Fuss and Henry Shapiro, trans. and ed.
Cambridge, Harvard University Press, 1971.

NUL   Nietzsche, Unpublished Letters. Kurt F.
Leidecker, ed. New York: Philosophical Library,
1959.

SLFN   Selected Letters of Friedrich Nietzsche.
Christopher Middleton, trans. and ed. Chicago:
University of Chicago Press, 1969.

Other Authors Referred to in Text

Alderman, Harold. Nietzsche's Gift. Athens, Ohio: Ohio
       University Press, 1977.

Barrett, William. Irrational Man. Garden City, New York:
       Doubleday Anchor Books, 1958.

Bok, Sissela. Lying, Moral Choice in Public and Private Life.
       New York: Vintage Books, 1978.

Brubacher, John S. A History of the Problems of Education,
       2nd ed. New York: McGraw-Hill, Inc., 1969.

Burgess, Charles. "Stanley G. Hall." In Encyclopedia of
       Education, Vol. 4. C. Deighton, ed. New York:
       The Macmillan Company and the Free Press, 1971,
       pp. 256-259.

Cole, Luella. A History of Education: A Social Interpretation.
       New York: Ronald Press, Co., 1959.

Copleston, Frederick. Nietzsche, Philosopher of Culture. New
    York: Barnes and Noble, 1975.

Danto, Arthur C. Nietzsche as Philosopher. New York: The
    Macmillan Company, 1965.

Deighton, Lee C., ed. The Encyclopedia of Education. New York:
    The Macmillan Co. and The Free Press, 1971.

Fischer, Kurt R. "Nazism as a Nietzschean 'Experiment'."
    Nietzsche-Studien, Band 6, 1977, pp. 116-122.

Good, H.G. A History of Education, A Social Interpretation.
    New York: Ronald Press Co., 1959.

Grimm, R.H. "Circularity and Self-Reference in Nietzsche."
    Metaphilosophy, Vol. 10, Nos. 3 and 4, July/October, 1979,
    pp. 289-305.

_____. Nietzsche's Theory of Knowledge. Berlin:
    Walter de Gruyter Press, 1976.

Haar, Michael. "Nietzsche and Metaphysical Language." In The
    New Nietzsche, David B. Allison, ed. New York: Dell
    Publishing Company, 1977, pp. 5-36.

Heidegger, Martin. Nietzsche, Vol. 1. David Farrell Krell,
    trans. San Francisco: Harper and Row, 1979.

Hill, Brian V. Education and the Endangered Individual.
    New York and London: Teachers College Press, Columbia
    University, 1973.

Hinman, Lawrence. "Nietzsche's Philosophy of Play." Philosophy
    Today, Vol. 18, No. 2/4, 1974, pp. 106-124.

Howey, Richard L. Heidegger and Jaspers on Nietzsche: An
    Examination of Heidegger's and Jaspers'
    Interpretations of Nietzsche. The Hague. Nijhoff,
    1973.

Jarrett, James L. Philosophy for the Study of Education.
    Boston: Houghton, Mifflin Company, 1969.

Kaufmann, Walter. Discovering the Mind, Vol. 2. New York:
    McGraw-Hill Book Co., 1980.

_____. Nietzsche, Philosopher, Psychologist,
    AntiChrist, 4th ed. Princeton, New Jersey: Princeton
    University Press, 1974.

Kaplan, Charles D. and Karl Weiglus. "Beneath Role Theory: Reformulating a Theory with Nietzsche's Philosophy." Philosophy and Social Criticism. Vol 6, No. 3, 1979, pp. 289–305.

Lampert, Laurence. "Zarathustra and his Disciples." Nietzsche-Studien, Band 8, 1979, pp. 309–333.

Magnus, Bernd. "Eternal Recurrence." Nietzsche-Studien, Band 8, 1979, pp. 362–377.

Mencken, H.L. The Philosophy of Friedrich Nietzsche. Port Washington, New York: Kennikat Press, 1908; reissue, 1967.

Mooney, Edward F. "Nietzsche and the Dance." Philosophy Today, Vol. 14, No. 1/4, Spring, 1970, pp. 38–43.

Perkinson, Henry J. Since Socrates: Studies in the History of Western Thought. New York: Longman, 1980.

Peters, H.F. Zarathustra's Sister. New York: Crown Publishers, 1977.

Plato. The Republic of Plato, Allan Bloom, trans. New York: Basic Books, Inc., 1968.

_____. The Laws, Trevor Saunders, trans. London: Penguin, 1970.

Power, Edward J. Main Currents in the History of Education. New York: McGraw-Hill, 1962, 1970.

Price, Kingsley. Education and Philosophical Thought. Boston: Allyn and Bacon, 1967.

Rusk, Robert. Doctrines of the Great Educators. New York: St. Martin's Press, 1979.

Sartre, Jean-Paul. Beaudelaire, Martin Turnell, trans. London: Penguin, 1970.

Solomon, Robert C. The Passions. Notre Dame: University of Notre Dame Press, 1976.

Valadier, Paul, "Dionysus versus the Crucified." In The New Nietzsche, David B. Allison, ed. New York: Dell Publishing Company, 1977, pp. 247–261.